CHILDHOOD

CHILDHOOD

JAN MYRDAL

Translated by
Christine Swanson

LAKE VIEW Press
Chicago

Library of Congress Cataloging-in-Publication Data

[Barndom. English]
Childhood / Jan Myrdal; translated by Christine Swanson.
192pp.
Originally published in Sweden as Barndom by P.A. Norstedt
& Söners Förlag, Stockholm, c1982.
ISBN 0-941702-29-4.
1. Myrdal, Jan—Biography—Youth. 2. Authors, Swedish—
20th century—Biography. I. Title.
PT9876.23.Y7B313   1991
838.7'374—dc20   91-26744
                                                       CIP

Lake View Press
P. O. Box 578279
Chicago, IL 60657

FOREWORD

Many readers of Jan Myrdal consider him a very Swedish writer, a man like Strindberg tortured by life and the complexity of his own being. This view is correct. Jan Myrdal has deeply confronted the dark urgings of his soul and the role of humanity in a possibly infinite universe.

But, as Myrdal reveals in *Childhood,* he is a boy as well as a man, a child of his times and his society and particularly of his family. Like any serious person, he has devoted much time trying to understand his early years and how he grew into adulthood.

It is his seriousness of purpose and resolute determination which give Myrdal's works their honesty and a truth which can be embarrassing and unexpectedly frank.

Few have tried so hard as Myrdal to understand themselves. At the center of this study lie his parents and his relationship with these Nobel prize winners, Gunnar and Alva Myrdal. It was, as the boy Jan saw it, a brutal relationship and in retrospect he convinces us that the boy was right. Not many children have survived a mother who saw her son as a kind of laboratory animal for behavioral studies and a father who did not conceal his contempt for the being he and his wife had brought into life.

But if Myrdal gives us excruciating scenes with an icy verisimilitude, he also gives us scenes of extraordinary warmth and love—the growing up of a boy who found in his grandparents surrogates suffused with humanity and common sense. With them Myrdal passed ideal days. This, no doubt, is why he survived.

Childhood can be read at many levels. To those who have known of Jan Myrdal's painfully impossible relations with his famous parents it provides a coda. When I first read his *Confessions of a Disloyal European,* I thought Jan had exaggerated, there seemed something polymorphous perverse about a middle-aged man coddling such violent reactions. After reading *Childhood* Myrdal's conduct seems natural. There is a harsh reality about *Childhood* that leaves little room for doubt of the trauma. And *Childhood* makes clear Myrdal's view of Sweden's separateness (and his own) from the Europe of Common Markets and common culture. Sweden is apart and away.

Myrdal's *Childhood* is no tale of boggy introspection. It is exciting and even funny, no chapter perhaps more tingling than his adventure on the winter icefloe, leaping from floe to floe, across the Karlberg Canal. Jan and his friends played this dangerous game many times. One morning he went out early. No one was around. The moon was still shining over Karlberg Palace. He missed a jump and went under the ice. To this day he has no recollection of how (or whether) he got out of the water. To this day he wonders whether he really did get out and how can he prove to himself that he is still alive.

This is the kind of question that might have entered Tom Sawyer's mind. It preoccupied the mind of the young Stockholm schoolboy and it still lingers there on cold dark nights of the long Swedish winter.

All his life Jan Myrdal has prided himself on being a maverick. Now this maverick has taken his place in the forefront of Swedish letters.

—HARRISON SALISBURY

PREFACE

In this my fifty-fifth year the watershed is behind me and the waters are now running downhill before me. Even if my strength is such that my life will be long, I have only a third—probably less or much less—of my lifetime left to dispose of. As I get older my strength inevitably begins to wane. It was in Berlin on the Kantstrasse one afternoon five years ago that I noticed I was no longer the one walking fastest through the city. I was used to passing everyone else. Because of that I preferred walking to taking the subway or a bus. But now when I thought I was walking at my usual pace, younger people went past me.

In the summer of 1981 I was supposed to go with the Cambodian guerrillas during the rainy season through the jungles down to Angkor and document the war against the Vietnamese occupiers in the temple zone. I had been there both before and during the last war and written about the temples. Then I was told that a Japanese filmmaker thirty years younger should try instead. It was a polite way of telling me I was getting too old. I don't know if he did go. I haven't seen any film about the fighting around Angkor.

There is much that I will no longer be able to do. I have accomplished the larger portion of my life's work. I don't like that thought. But it is true. It is time to look back. How have I become what I am?

In another political and personal turning point in life, I found it necessary to check my bearings and wrote *The*

Confessions of a Disloyal European. It belongs together with *Childhood.* It can be read as the first volume of a series.

I usually say and write that I act consciously with full insight into both my open and my hidden motives; that intellectual work demands awareness and politics is a conscious activity. Even in apparently irrational acts and in the midst of overwhelming emotional currents of hate or love, I hold that it is both possible and necessary to consciously reach and hold on to this insight. You should be transparent before your own gaze. You should know your darkest and most hidden urges and thoughts. Though there is no need to share that knowledge with others.

But long before I was able to act consciously—not to speak of publicly taking strongly controversial positions—after correcting for that irrational and emotional drift that always affects the course, I had already been formed as a person. That identity had been formed which since then has determined the way I act and react in love and in work as in politics and art; that identity which guides both waking work and nighttime dream-life.

How did I become that person?

I write, then, about a childhood. I am not writing an autobiography. The text does not pretend to be true confessions, objective and thus false as a police protocol. I write my words. The childhood I depict is mine. People who want to prove that "those doors open inward and not outward," and that "that painting was hung there and not there," and that "it was then and not then," can of course entertain themselves with such questions the way people entertain themselves with crosswords and playing solitaire. But that does not concern me and has nothing to do with the text. This is a prose story like *Confessions of a Disloyal European.*

During this childhood an *I* was formed. Later the identity of that *I* would determine the intellectual awakening during the great leap from childhood to adolescence. Childhood is a determinant. Forming the personality that later will react and act. But the great intellectual awakening during the emotional upheaval of becoming a grownup during puberty is not included in this text. That belongs to a later phase of becoming an individual, the years beyond thirteen.

Now this year when this story is being written, my eldest grandson is about as old as that child I now will describe. In that year fifty years ago my grandfather and his whole life was of great importance to me; was a part of me. He was born April 4, 1876. Thus in one sense this story spans more than a century. It is a century of great events. The childhood I describe was shaped also by these changes but I am not writing a social chronicle. In *Childhood* events before and during the thirties are taken as given, as are the houses and forests and streets. Given as the barges are to the boy looking at them passing in the canal outside his window.

The reasoned description of social changes belongs to another story. One I might later write. The society and the social relations that are taken as given by the child become truly visible after puberty.

And so I now return to Stockholm a couple of years after the great Stockholm exhibition of 1930. The exhibition that was said to herald the new and modern times in Europe. A new era of sun and light and air and frankness and modernity in European town-planning and architecture; in art, life and politics.

At that time in our history I begin with a boy running in the dark.

—*JAN MYRDAL*

CHILDHOOD

CHAPTER 1

Fifty years ago I am running through the apartment in the night and dark. When I come out into the corridor the glass doors stand wide open into the dining room. The parquet floor is cold under the soles of my feet. It is newly polished. Inside the floor shines under three windows. The ceiling is white. The yellow raw silk drapes are completely still. Under the window there are six black chairs with loose cushions of yellow leather. They stand in a row. The room is lit up. It is filled with a cool light from the street outside the windows. When I reach toward the chairs I am able to look out. I am five going on six. It is late winter in the year 1933 in Stockholm.

When I went to bed in the evening I knew that I would soon be wide awake and have to run. I ran every night. The last thing I did in the evening was to clear a broad path through my room from the bed in the corner to the door. I put away the books and the toys. I didn't want to stumble in the darkness when I began to run.

It's dark in the apartment. The darkness is clammy and cold. Every step takes time as it does when you walk in the night. The darkness acts as a check. When I open the door from my room the doorknob clicks a little. The hinges squeak slightly. There in the corridor lay the toilet to the right and farther away is the hall. They are both in the middle of the house. The kitchen and Mary's room face the street. Mary is the housekeeper. "Maid" is not said here. To the left the parents have their suite with bedroom and study and sitting room and bathroom and balcony. I can distinguish between right and left. The normal eye is to the right and the other eye is to the left.

I don't turn on any lights when I run in the night. I don't touch the switches and I don't call and I don't say anything because people can wake up around me. I am not supposed to be running.

When I must get out of the darkness, I try to reach the window in the dining room before time runs out and get up on a chair. Then I can look out. Everything out there is very clear. The world stands still. Everything is there. The street lamps shine. I can see the street below me and the trees beyond and the quay and the canal. If there were moonlight I would also see Karlberg palace. And then farther out toward the right and into the city St. Erik's bridge and all the many houses. There are windows that shine. Sometimes the lights go out.

I ran at night the whole spring and the following fall into the winter. It is snowing out there and everything I see is white cones under the street light and I can see the big flakes that come out of darkness toward me. In the spring the sky is completely glass green. Then the houses are dark. When the night is black there are circles of light on the street and trees. There is ice on the canal and the ice is blue and there is snow and there is open water and the moon twinkles on the water and it is so black that I can hardly see where the canal begins.

Sometimes a car drives by. I can hear it come. I can follow it with my eyes when it comes in under the house. Sometimes a person wanders down below. It can be a couple. They move slowly across the street. Everything is very clear and very commonplace. I get on my knees and look down at the street or I sit and look out over the canal and there is a lot to see. No one sees me and I do not look in toward the apartment.

Before I need to run I lie in my bed in my room and the room is full of darkness. They put me on the floor and stand around me and question me and then they say that I don't explain why I run. But that's not true. I have tried to explain but they don't understand. They wanted me to say something different. Something they told me to say. I stand there and they go back and forth on each side of me and want me to say that I run because I'm afraid of the dark and anxious. Then they tell me why I'm afraid of the dark and anxious. If I say what they want me to say I get to go out and play. But I refuse to say it because it isn't true. I don't say anything. I look away from them. They walk back and forth, but I look away from them and it is like the way the pendulum goes back and forth in grandmother's Mora clock. Their voices continue around me but I change the voices to the clock's tick-tock tick-tock. In the end I am left in peace.

One day I tried to explain what the darkness in my room is like before I get up and begin running. But it was not what they wanted me to say so they didn't hear it.

My room has windows facing the garden. The windows are in the middle of the wall. When I stand with my back to the window my bed is in the corner to my right. Straight ahead is the door to the hall. At night when the light is out and it is dark I like to see pictures up above me in the corner of the ceiling on the left. I call down the pictures I want to see and then they change themselves. I don't let them come too near me. I hold them about three feet from the wall, right under the ceiling. Sometimes the pictures can be frightening. But I'm not really afraid of them. They're not dangerous. They can't come any closer.

I can call them down. But it is difficult to handle them and I can't just put them away again. For example, I call down a pirate with a red beard and bare head. There's the head. It talks but nothing can be heard. The eyes roll. It is savage and shakes itself. There's a knife between the teeth, but I can't put it away. I want to put it away and call down another picture, but then it gapes more and more. It doesn't have a knife. One eye is completely white, but it cannot see. The other eye is closed up. The mouth gapes more and more. Maybe someone's strangling him. Then it is gone. Then I make an aquarium in the corner to the left. I am not allowed to have an aquarium. They make ugly water spots on the parquet floor, they say. But now I have an aquarium up there. Tall green plants. Small fishes swim among the growth. I make them different colors. Yellow, red, green and black. There are stones in the aquarium. It is beautiful. One of the yellow fishes is big. It grows larger and larger. It flounders and hits and grabs at the small fishes trying to escape. But the big yellow fish swallows them one after the other. Then the whole thing disappears again.

I can call down whole people too. I can call down Grandfather if I want, or Grandmother or whomever I want. But I don't call down anyone I don't want.

I once said something about a pirate with a red beard, but I didn't get to say much. They told me right away that he was the reason I was running at night. They said I was afraid of him. But that wasn't it. The head came forward sometimes by itself too, but it couldn't come out of its corner. Sometimes someone strangled him so the eyes became almost like eggs and stuck out from the head. It could be fearsome when you looked at it. And it didn't work to just close the eyes, either. He was there whether I closed my eyes or not. And if I turned away he was still there and I could see him even if he was behind my head. He could not get away and it was scary to look at him but in a strange way that made the stomach tingle and it almost tickled.

No, it wasn't the pictures that made it necessary to run. It was something else. Things happened in the dark. The room grew very large. The ceiling disappeared high above me and went away into emptiness. The dark was a big empty block. My thoughts became a kind of moving block. They were in me and around me and over me and I breathed them in. It was like sinking under the water. I couldn't explain this. There were no words to describe the darkness. I lay in my bed and thought a word and the word was there. It could be high or low. It could be flat or heavy or yellow or red, but it was there. One word shot in over the other and the words built pyramids and mountains and whole landscapes. But the colors were not normal colors and the ceiling disappeared into the great emptiness and the walls began to fall out and the floor began to fall away and I had to go to the door quickly before everything just blew away and whirled down. I didn't talk about that. There were no words for that and they didn't understand my words.

Outside the windows here in the dining room the world is completely still. The street lights shine over the trees. Branches sprawl in the winter because there are no leaves left. I look at the tree. I close my eyes and I open my eyes and it's the same tree that stands in the same place and looks just the same. A man comes walking and he goes slowly one step after another. And when I look I know he's still out there and continues to walk even though I close my eyes. I count the steps he takes when I close my eyes and he takes a step and he takes a new step and he takes a third step and he takes a fourth step. When I open my eyes and look at him he has taken four steps forward on the street and now the fifth and the tree is the same tree as before I closed my eyes. I look at that. I look at branch after branch. Street lights shine bright on the branches and they are very clear.

I know how the room looks behind me. There is light in it from the street lamps. But I don't need to turn around to see that. I don't want to, either. There stands the table. The legs are black but the top is yellow. On the table there is a little yellow cloth. It is a fine cloth of thick shiny material. On the cloth is a white vase. It is shaped like a woman's hand holding a vase. The hand's nails are pointed and one can see thin veins on the back of the hand. They are not blue. The whole hand is white and made of stone that is almost transparent. In the vase is a red rose. It is made of fabric and wire. The leaves are thick and smooth and made of wax paper. The rose shines behind me.

I get on my knees on the chair. If I look down I can see the seat of the chair and the floor. In the corner to the right against the wall is the low white bookcase. It stretches into the dining room. In the bookcase are art books. On the bookcase stands a large cactus. It has long pointy spikes. They are like long sewing needles. Above the bookcase toward the door there hangs a painting. It is not large. It has a black frame. The frame sticks out so far that you feel as if you're standing in a window when you look at the painting. But the window is black. The painting shows a man walking in a landscape. At the left in the landscape is a white house with a flat roof. The man is black but has a gold shadow almost surrounding him. There is green grass in the landscape. It was bought at an exhibition of young painters, the Halmstad group. It was not painted on canvas, but on wood. You can knock on the double man.

On the wall behind me, behind glass, in a narrow black frame, is a drawing of a thin man with glass eyes. The man has long thin fingers and looks melancholy. It is Kokoshka's portrait of Karl Kraus, I know now. Beside that, right next to the door toward the parents' suite is a stack of black chairs. They're used when many guests come. They stand on top of each other and when you look through the backs they are like a little movie theater. I can stand there and pretend to be at the movies and there is row after row down toward the screen.

The architect Sven Markelius designed the chairs. He comes sometimes to visit the parents. He has given me a house too. It is a model of a collective house. It has silver paper panes in the windows. Inside the house is a marble. You can hear the marble roll when you shake the collective house, but it's not possible to see inside the house. It is blind. It looks like a real house with a chimney and round columns at the entrance. There is a sidewalk and everything. But it's made of paper and has no color.

When I get on my knees and look out over the canal in the night I cannot see the other bank but I know how it looks there. The black chairs with the yellow leather seats I'm standing on were at the Stockholm exhibition. Almost everything in the front room and in the parents' suite has been at the Stockholm exhibition or comes from Svenskt Tenn, the exclusive and modern furniture shop.

It's cold in the room and I'm actually chilled. I'd like to go to the toilet too because I've started to shiver but I don't even want to turn around because the glass doors are wide open to the corridor.

I wake up when Mary shakes me. It is morning and all the lamps are lit. Now the window has become black because outside it's still night. She sighs and says:

"Have you done it again?"

I was not able to get through the darkness to the toilet and while I slept I pissed on myself.

Everything shows on these cushions. Now she has dried the leather cushions. Now she changes them. Now they all look just as nice again, even though I have made spots on four of them. I wash myself and brush my teeth. Then I dress myself. I can dress myself. I fasten the long brown stockings to the one-piece undergarment. I don't need any help. Afterward I sit in the kitchen and eat cereal with milk. I get to have a sandwich with salted cod roe too. Mary fixes coffee trays for the parents. She makes rolls of butter and lays them in a pyramid. She puts the English marmalade on the tray. She toasts bread and brews coffee. We don't boil coffee like others do. We brew coffee. Then she puts on her serving apron and serving cap. She gets the papers, *Dagens Nyheter* and *Socialdemokraten,* and lays them on the tray and then she goes into the parents' suite. It is seven o'clock and I hear her knock. She tells them about me. I hear the parents' voices. They sound excited. I go into my room. I hope they don't come to talk to me.

CHAPTER 2

In January 1934 when I had stopped running at night and Grandfather was already dead, I had stained all six chair cushions. I had even stained the clean sides which had been turned up. I can't remember what they said to me on the days they discovered I had been up in the night. I only see their eyes move. Gunnar got blue veins in his forehead. It throbbed. It was not as if I wanted to piss on myself or even did it every night. I did it when I was cold, I think. From Gesta, I was accustomed to getting up in the night to piss. It was no different from having Vichy water on the night table and waking up at night to drink it. Grandfather did it. Grandmother did it and I did it. We did it at home at Gesta and I continued here at Kungsholmsstrand. But here I ran too. In January 1934 when Grandfather had died and I stopped running, they took the cushions off the chairs and had them dyed. They were dyed red. That spring the Matisse was hung on the wall as well. A lithography or a reproduction. I haven't seen it in a long time. A woman with a flower, I remember. A red flower.

I still have the chairs. I took them over in the move in 1955. Otherwise the chairs would have been thrown out. By then the color on the cushions had become old and worn. The shiny covers had cracked. I had the chairs at Skånegatan. Gun put slipcovers over the cushions. Blue and white checked cotton. It was what we had on hand. When A died we took the chairs to Fagervik. She sat on one when she committed suicide. When I called she was already dead on it and the police were there. Now the cushions have new covers. Now they are orange

Manchester velvet.

Two of the chairs are in the kitchen. We sit on them when we eat. The other four are extra chairs. They are in the dining room. Two stand on either side of the bureau against the wall in the living room. Two stand under the three Japanese woodblock prints on the inner wall against Gun's studio. When the children come or when we have guests, we take the two chairs into the kitchen. There is also one of the stackable chairs designed by Sven Markelius. That one I've had since the forties. It has no cushion so we can climb on it when we need something from the top cupboard. If we are more than five at the table we eat in the dining room. If we set the table for more than six people, we take in the extra chairs. We don't like to have dinners for more than eight people at the table. It's best with six. We have seldom had ten and only a few times twelve. One time we had fifteen sitting at the table. In the years at the end of the sixties and the beginning of the seventies we used to have family dinners the day after Christmas. Since then we have usually been on a trip in the winter. The day after Christmas 1970 both children were here, both of my uncles with their wives, a cousin with her husband and a cousin with wife and children. We ate and talked. The cousins stayed a long time. They didn't leave until three o'clock in the morning.

When I look up from the typewriter it is still night. In the window I can see myself. The gold-bowed eyeglasses shine. The face and body come forward in dark colors through the window's reflection against the night. Around me in the picture and behind my head, bookcases with books. There is light from the work lamp. Far behind me and high above me in the background, lifted on its Empire pedestal in black and gold, the plaster of Paris head of Aphrodite. She looks down at me and in the dark reflection you can't see that her eyes are white and dead. The companion piece, "Klytia," portrait of Antonia, mother of Claudius Caesar, is hidden behind the pushed-out bookcases. It was Uncle Folke who brought them.

"They fit in your house," he said. They were cast about 1840. Many things here in the house come from him. The dining room table and the large clock and the secretary by the TV set, for example. Not just furniture, of course. The large copper washtub I use for a wastepaper basket comes from him as well as numerous porcelain and decorative objects. I liked him a lot. He almost never spoke to me when I was a child. I just followed him together with the dogs. When he got angina pectoris and became pensive he decided to take his life so he would not have to lie sick. Gun and I were in China. It was 1976 and Gun was in a TB sanatorium in Tsingtao. He wrote to me then. He didn't usually do that. I think it was the first time he ever wrote to me. He wondered when I was coming home. The trip home was delayed because Gun was sick for a long time. When we finally got home in the winter we visited him. He mentioned that he was not doing well. Otherwise we talked mostly about provincial Södermanland metalwork. When I left he gave me something he had long intended to give me, he said; something unusual. A pair of carved wooden hames crowned with the heads of mountain cocks. The carving had a crude power.

"The nobility came driving from the big estates. Their carriages were fine, with richly decorated harnesses. The farmers didn't want their harnesses to be less ornate, so they carved harnesses in beautiful colors to use when they drove to church."

As we walked he took my hand and said goodbye. I said we would meet soon. He was supposed to come over. But he didn't answer. After we left he made the final arrangements. Then he took the car and drove out into the woods to the south and shot himself. He had waited for months so he could see me one more time again before he did that. He was afraid he would get worse and be hospitalized and lose his freedom and I had taken a long time to get home.

When he died, he left everything in order. He would have been able to save up pills and take them. He hadn't wanted to do that, he wrote, because that could have caused trouble for the doctor who prescribed them. He had also been looking a long time for an appropriate place. One doesn't want to die by a rubbish heap. He was an outdoorsman and a hunter. As a child I used to go across the fields from Gesta over to Kvicksta, traipsing after him with the dogs when he went into the woods to hunt. When Grandfather was forced to sell Kvicksta in 1940 because both uncles were called up and there wasn't even anyone to help with the garden, Folke kept the hunting rights. But Grandfather built a house for himself and kept it when the farm was sold. The house was sold when Grandfather died in the autumn of 1942. That summer I had lived there with him and read. He was a big one for Strindberg and advised me also to read Frank Norris. *Octopus* and *The Pit* were among his favorites. Naturalism in this period of North American culture fascinated him just as he was fascinated by Zola. His taste was formed by Social Democratic educational thought around the turn of the century. He was a teetotaler and an atheist and in politics he had been a Social Democrat but became an Agrarian when he had earned enough as a builder so he could buy a respectable farm. He had been anti-Nazi the whole time. After he retired he became a socialist again. In the evenings of 1942 he listened to Radio Moscow. Of everyone I knew, he is the one who most resembles Stalin. The same nose, the same mustache, the same look.

Folke's sister, my mother Alva, was not invited to his funeral. He himself had decided that my parents should not be allowed to come. The last time they saw each other was when Folke still had his antique shop at the entrance to Eskilstuna. He had always been interested in antiques. He specialized in Sörmland metalwork and locks. He worked a lot at the Eskilstuna museum and was a good friend of Karl Braunerhielm, the curator there. After the war he had shared a car dealership with a friend. When the partner retired and the business was sold, Folke turned entirely to old locks and his collections. He also opened an antique shop so he could buy and sell the things he collected. Gunnar and Alva came into the shop. Gunnar took a look around and said:

"So, here you sit in your little booth."

Then he laughed. And Alva also laughed. But not Folke.

It was my Uncle Stig who called to tell me that Folke had shot himself. I was standing in the doorway to the workroom when the telephone rang. I could see straight out over Gripsholmsviken and over to Mariefred. I could see the house from which Stig was calling. He said that Folke had shot himself. Everything was quiet around me then. Before I had a chance to see Stig again he was already dead. He got up the evening after and went out to the kitchen and died there. And Alva wasn't invited to his funeral either.

Everyone in the family who liked me is now dead. Everyone except Aunt Elsa, who is still alive. She is 81. Uncles Gustav and Gösta are dead. Uncles Folke and Stig are dead. Grandfather is dead. Grandmother is dead. My other grandmother and grandfather are dead. I liked them a lot. Especially my mother's father. My mother's mother was eccentric. She was always someplace else, even if she was in the room. She was sickly for 25 years. Before she left to visit her daughter Rut she took out Grandfather's funeral clothes and put them in order. "You'll need them," she said to me. She traveled to Nibble at

Tillberga. There she laid down on the bed and died. Grandfather died there too. He had gone there to catch crayfish in the stream with Rut and Elon. He pulled a large female from the net and said he had got hold of a big one. Then he fell forward and was dead. I liked them both, but I never believed they really liked me. They didn't stand up for me. I was a grandchild, nothing more. Among their grandchildren, Ulla was probably the most important to them. She was oldest in that branch. She was a half year older than I. In my branch I was the oldest.

Gun woke me up about three in the morning.

"You are making such strange noises," she said.

Since I was awake anyway she wanted me to go downstairs. I was supposed to turn off the outdoor lights and check the pot with the moose leg. It had been set on slow cook since the afternoon. But when I came out into the upstairs hall and started to go down I saw them and it was very cold inside me. I couldn't go. After a time I turned around and went back to the bedroom.

"Did you go down?," she asked.

"No," I said. Then she went back to sleep and after a while I got up to work.

I had not turned on the lamp in the hall when I stood at the steps and was going to go down. When I took the first step I looked down into the house as if a lid had been lifted off and I could see down into the room. It was dark down there, but I saw them sitting on the chairs. I sat completely still and saw their faces very clearly. In the kitchen sat Grandfather and Grandmother, each on a chair. The cat lay on his pillow in the window and looked at them. The cat's eyes were shining as animal eyes do in the dark. Grandfather and Grandmother sat at the kitchen table and both of them looked straight at me. But I should not have been able to see them. They sat so I should only have been able to see their necks. But I saw them plainly before me looking at me. In the dining room sat Gustav and Gösta on either side of the bureau. They had their hands on their knees and looked straight ahead. Under the three Japanese actors' portraits on the inner wall toward Gun's studio sat Folke and Stig. Even though it was completely dark in the house I could see them down there in the two rooms. They waited. I could not go down to them. I was completely cold and turned and went back into the bedroom.

Later, when I went down to work, everything was as usual and the cat came out and rubbed himself against me when I sat down for coffee. He wanted to have butter. He always gets butter in the morning while I have coffee before work. I had tuned the little short-wave radio to the BBC and put on the headset so as not to wake up the house when I listened to the news and drank morning coffee. When I went through the dining room later on my way to the workroom the cat followed me. He hopped up and laid himself on one of the chairs under the Japanese woodblock prints. From there he has an overview of the house. He is 16 years old now and doesn't catch fieldmice or housemice, except on a few rare occasions.

CHAPTER 3

Childhood is a deep and lasting shame. Like sour beer, it leaves an aftertaste. One winter evening in 1961 Gun and I were at the home of Gunilla and Otto Rathsman in New Delhi. We were often with them. It was a beautiful cool evening. We were discussing economic development work. We didn't entirely agree, but we weren't having an argument. Why should we do that? I can't remember that we ever had one. People can see things differently without getting into a quarrel.

We were talking about Ulla Lindström. Together with Erlander and Sträng and Lange she was part of a newly formed working group for international assistance issues in the cabinet. Someone, maybe Gun, maybe Gunilla, mentioned her father, political economist and Farmers' Association politician Nils Wohlin. To my own astonishment I came out with a bitter attack on the deceased general director of customs.

"That's just how he was, he and his child," I said.

The outburst was incomprehensible. Even to me. I didn't have the slightest cause to think ill of Nils Wohlin and had barely met Ulla Lindström. I considered her to be only moderately talented and a weak politician, but that's not the kind of judgment that usually causes outbursts of deep emotion. After a moment of confusion we continued the discussion of assistance questions and the Indian economy.

When we drove home to the Defense Colony in the evening, Gun asked:

"What was the matter with you? What was it with Wohlin?"

I was irritated and had a hard time falling asleep. But I must have fallen asleep because after a while I was ice cold wide awake. Gun is asleep. I hear her breathing. It is quiet. And in front of me I see it all again as if it were being played out in a huge bubble, some kind of floating bowl like a globe-shaped goldfish aquarium, and I hear voices. It is February 1933 at Lidingö. We walk on the sand path and are coming from the Wohlins'.

"Why don't we talk about this now, Jan?" says Alva.

Her voice is cold and blonde and flutelike, high above me in Hiserud's winter. I am five years old. I know that. I can say it more precisely than that. Jan is five years, six months and three weeks old, I answer when anyone asks how old I am. One doesn't say "I." One says "Jan." It sounds better coming from a child.

It's winter. I take Alva's hand. She holds it out. I kiss her hand and say:

"Forgive Jan for being so naughty."

We had been visiting Margit Wohlin. She was married to Nils Wohlin at the time and was the daughter of Gunnar's teacher and mentor and supporter, his old professor Gustav Cassel. I was supposed to play with the daughter, Anna, while the grownups talked. Anna was four years old. But it didn't go well. I yelled and laughed loudly and stomped on the floor and behaved badly. I created a disturbance.

"We have to be able to talk calmly and rationally about such things," said Alva.

"Jan will never do it again. Jan is nice."

"Now we shall discuss the matter," said Alva.

The discussion continued all the way home to Kungsholmsstrand. She spoke to me while we sat in the streetcar. I cried. But I cried inside and silently so no one would hear. Such a thing should not be heard.

"Poor Jan. He must be so sorry," she said.

When we got home I said:

"Jan can call and apologize."

"Does Jan really think he can explain himself in the right way on the telephone?"

"Jan is sorry. Jan really is sorry."

"Wouldn't it be better if we wrote a letter in which Jan asks forgiveness for his behavior? Jan can dictate for me and I will write now. What does Jan want me to write? Think it over carefully!"

"Pardon Jan for being so naughty," I said.

"Yes, I shall write, 'Please pardon Jan for being a little bit naughty.' Does Jan agree to that? What else shall I write?"

"If they come over here Jan will never again be naughty."

She sat at the desk in the parents' suite. I stood on the floor in front of the desk and watched her write. When she had written a while she was done. She folded the paper and took out an envelope. She wrote the address on the envelope, put the letter inside, licked the envelope closed and put a stamp on it. Then she gave me the letter.

"Now Jan himself will go to the mailbox with this letter and put it in. Then Jan will really have apologized."

Mary helped me with my coat. It was a teddy-bear coat. I put my cap on. I fumbled with the bootlace so Mary helped me. I held the letter in my right hand and walked down the steps. I pretended there was nothing outside the stairway and sang.

"And so we go down the steps and so we go down the steps."

But I sang to myself in case someone came and heard.

When I was back upstairs Mary made a cup of hot chocolate for me. I got a roll too. Then I went through the hall to my room. When I opened my door I heard the parents talking in their suite. Gunnar had come home while I was downstairs with the letter.

"Our unruly youngster was soft as wax afterward," said Alva. "He was terribly upset and apologized."

I pulled the door closed behind me and stood in my room. Now I didn't hear them any more. It was already evening and dark even though it wasn't late. When I looked out at the yard I could see light in the windows across the way. Darkness crept up through the floor and stepped into the room behind me. Everything was very far away and I wasn't sad or anything. The glass was cold and felt good against my forehead and I said:

"Now we are waiting for nightfall."

CHAPTER 4

That spring I went to a Montessori school. There you were supposed to play with other children under the Montessori teacher's supervision. You were supposed to walk in a circle and wave your hands and stamp your feet. My only strong memory of that school is the wonderful glass-clear blue spring days when the ice broke up and the sun shone in broad streaks on the dining room floor. The parents were away and I got to skip Montessori school and play. That was Tuesdays.

On Tuesdays *Allers* came. We had *Allers* at Gesta. Here at Kungsholmsstrand the parents had *Idun* and *Veckojournalen* and then *Morgonbris* and such things. Grandfather had *Vårt Hem*. But on Tuesdays *Allers* came. Then Mary let me have the sniffles and I could stay home. When the parents had gone I could hear Mary sing. I got up and washed and dressed myself. Then I jumped down the stairs and passed the flowerbeds on my way to the tobacco shop where I bought *Allers*.

I lay on my stomach in the dining room and read. There was sun in the room and for lunch Mary made baked eggs with pan-fried sausages. I don't know now whether I read or just paged through the magazine spelling and counting the letters. But because I didn't let anyone read to me or take me on their knee and pat me on the head and help me read *Allers*, I must have learned to spell by myself and put things together and understand. In *Allers* I read about the phases of the moon and about the moon and all the planets and about Captain Willy's adventure. And about how to build models and what to do with a fretsaw. I can date those reading experiences to 1933 because Alva was busy with child psychology and that subject included studies in children's lives. Sometimes when I was at home she sat and looked at me and made notes about what I said and dated the notes. About 1933 she documented my fantasy life and the stories I drew and told. She sat behind me so I wouldn't see her or be disturbed when I fantasized. I heard the pen scrape against the paper behind me, but I continued to talk anyway. I used to do that.

"The way you talk is enough to make one crazy," said Mary. "The mouth on you goes all day long like a mill." But she smiled when she said that. Because of that I talked even when Alva sat there behind me and studied me. I remember the stories from 1933. When I read them again I notice how Alva understood only certain sentences. Or maybe I told them only in short versions for her. I was careful. Mary had heard them in a different way. But I repeat them as they were noted.

1. There was a sailor who was going out to sail for the last time. An hour after they set out the boat sprang a leak. They steered with a functionalistic cord and the guy who tended the fire stamped on a drill and punched it right through the bottom. Soon there was nothing to see of the big ship except foam.

For that story I made three drawings, one of them I described.

Boat with rudder, flag, keel and fish in the water. Now the boat has sunk this deep.

The third picture I did not describe. It was a cemetery with gravestones for dead sailors.

2. The pilot was locked in a prison tower but above him there was a rather big hole to fly out of. He flew out like nothing. Then he flew away so the witch would not see

the kid who was with him and the guy who flew. He flew
to France and he flew down to London. There he went
into a cafe and drank coffee. He left there after an hour.

For that story I made a drawing of an airport seen from the
air, with hangars and planes. I explained that was the airport.

3. The story about the petrified man. He went first to a
petrified land and then he came to a big petrified doctors'
place. That means there are only doctors in long rows.
Then he went down a petrified pit. There he became petrified. When he came up he saw the petrified house of
parliament. Then he left the petrified land. He saw a farm
there where he asked to lay down.

For that story I drew a pit seen from the air and the facade
of a house under which I wrote "palace" with uneven and
sprawling letters.

4. There was a boy who liked to roam. He began to roam.
He didn't get any further than the fence when he felt a little hungry. Then he went on toward the woods and
thought he would catch something to eat there. But he
could only get hold of two lingonberries. Then he found
three blueberries and then he went further into the wood
and there he found five lingonberries and five blueberries.
He went further into the wood and he was proud of being
gone away. Then he came across a little cabin to lay down
in. He found a little rabbit for company and so he stayed
away forever.

5. There was an O who was going to travel to Africa and
so he came to Stockholm. He went to the king's palace
and later he went on an Atlantic steamer to an island. It
had been deserted before but now it would be fully occu-

pied. Then he built himself a house. The people saw it was not a good island so they went back on the steamer. But he stayed there forever.

For that story there are two pictures.

The O with people. This drawing depicts a huge meadow, a rectangle where an O with head and legs and feet goes around. Next to the O are eight triangles without heads, arms, legs or bodies.

The steamer leaves the deserted island. From the air you see the steamer with a Swedish flag and much smoke.

> 6. There was a carrot who was supposed to go away from the earth. First he went to South America and stayed there overnight. Then he went to South Africa and then he went away from the earth. Then he landed on a new planet and then he went away from that planet and landed on the next planet and continued as long as the sky continued.

For that story there are three pictures.

Three earths with stars above and planets.

The carrot. It is flaming red.

The third picture depicts many planets against a winter street with stars.

I don't think Alva understood much of what I said. Nobody did. I knew that. In the afternoons when *Allers* had been thoroughly read and Mary was busy with lunch, I stood at the kitchen window and looked out over the canal. I saw a tugboat towing a train of barges loaded with gravel through the canal. I had been telling Mary about Africa and now she said:

"They might be sailing toward the warm South."

"Sure," I said. "And if they sail long enough they'll have to keep on sailing toward the warm North."

"Don't talk nonsense," she said.

I watched the barges as they drew away under St. Erik's bridge and Mary didn't understand that the Earth was round either.

Afterward I lay on the floor and drew with crayons on the tablet. I lay under the kitchen table so as not to be in Mary's way.

"What are you drawing?" she asked.

"A cabinet with beds," I said.

"But it doesn't look like a box bed," said Mary.

"I'm drawing that we lay in it and dreamed that the closet had golf knickers," I said.

She was busy setting the table for the two of us on the table above me. The parents would eat later in the dining room. Guests were coming. Then I drew mechanical birds. Then I drew birds dreaming about a goblin.

"Soon you can see what the bird imagined the goblin did," I said.

Then I drew a big picture in red and blue and yellow and black. It was the bird's dream, a goblin who only wanted to do people harm. The goblin's name was Stoneleg. He carried a sack. In the goblin's face you could see what he wanted. The mouth was incredibly blue and the eyes black surrounded by yellow. But so you could really understand I drew a round circle at the goblin's feet. The circle was blue. There I drew the letter O and the letter N. On the next sheet I showed the cage the goblin lived in. There were yellow bars. Then the goblin got into the airplane. The mechanical bird woke up and imagined he had become entirely different. You could see that because now when you looked at him from the front he had large feathers on his head. Then I drew how the mechanical bird thought the earth was round and that he lived on the side.

"Now lunch is ready," said Mary.

CHAPTER 5

When the boat arrived at Stallarholmen Grandfather was waiting. He had a Buick. It was black and you could see yourself in the paint. When we drove home to Gesta I sat next to him and saw the trees reflected on the hood of the car as we drove through the woods. He was sick now.

They tried to get me to say "At home in Stockholm." But I didn't do that. I said "At home at Gesta." They didn't like that. When I drew I drew people and trains and nursery school with all the children. If I drew rooms I preferred to make floor plans so you could see where the table was and where the chairs were. You could see the children in the nursery school from above like small circles. But if I drew a house I drew Gesta. I drew the big house and I drew the playhouse which Grandfather built for me. He was a building contractor, actually, and could have built whatever he wanted. He designed a playhouse for me. He designed a table and built-in benches and he designed an elevator and everything, just like a real one, only smaller. Then he said:

"Let's build it, shall we?"

He had it built. He had a carpentry shop at Gesta, where all of the wooden chairs and things were made. The playhouse was built and it stood in the yard and had a black key. It was red with white trim and white window frames because it had real glass windows. The playhouse was mine. I played in it when I was at home.

He was sick now. He got raw eggs. He made holes in them and sucked out the egg. I was afraid he would die. No one said that to me and no one talked about his illness when I was present but I had been afraid he would die ever since last winter.

"Yes, that's the way it goes," he said.

It was one of the first years after we got Fagervik and moved home to Sweden. That would have been about 1965. Gun was in Mariefred to shop. She had gone to Curt Ohlsson who had a radio shop on the square. She was going to ask about our antenna. There was an old man there. Everyone talked and joked. When the man was about to leave Curt Ohlsson said:

"You don't know who you were talking with just now. That was the wife of Gesta-Pelle's grandson."

"Damn," said the old man and looked at Gun.

Grandfather had been dead for more than forty years then but it was the same when we were going to add on to the house. We needed a studio and a workroom and a library and a darkroom and things. It was a really big addition. We needed to take a good-sized loan. The bank's appraiser came out to see us and look at the house. We drank coffee. He began to talk about Grandfather. He had known him. Grandfather had sat on the bank's board of directors. It was he who took the initiative for Gripsholm's people's high school. A people's high school was needed in northern Södermanland, he thought. He believed in the idea of the people's high school too. He was self-taught and he'd had to go the long way. He'd had only an evening course in drawing when he and a friend became building contractors and got the contract for station houses up through Dalarna. He came here to Gesta in 1922. He had made money in the black market during the war. He traded and bought farms and sold them at a profit. Now he had bought a manor with farmhands and everything and was called a squire. I lay on the leather sofa in the office at home at Gesta when he tapped out his "Memo re: the institution of a people's high school in northern Södermanland" on the rattling typewriter. "The Swedish people's high school has shown itself to be a strong living power."

He was patriotic. He sang when he was in the mood. He threw out his hands and sang.

"Proud flame against dark skies."

Then he became serious and emotional. He always raised the flag himself at the flagpole in the yard in front of the house. He was a prime mover on the highway board and when the conservatives in Livgedinget judicial district came out with the farmers and businessmen slate during the 1930 county council election, he was the third name for Åkers and Selebo jurisdictional district.

Leaseholder J. Alder. Länna.
Juror Gottfried Andersson. Hyndevad.
Estate owner C.A. Pettersson. Gesta, Toresund.
Factory manager Ernst Sundell. Åkers Styckebruk.
Gardener W. Löweberg. Strängnäs.
Administrator D. Isaksson. Hässelbyholm.
Accountant Oskar Karlson. Åkers Styckebruk.
Farmer Sven Brunfors. Brunna, Häradsvik.
Farmer C. Björkén. Fjällsta, Stallarholm.

He had raised himself up out of poverty. Now he had a gold signet ring and smoked cigars and a heavy silver watch chain draped across his stomach. He was sick. He sat at the desk in the office and I lay on the leather sofa and drew. It was summer. He had taken a card out of the drawer. He looked at it. Then he called to me.

"Come here," he said.

I looked at the photo he held out. I had seen it before. I used to take out the drawers and look at the old photos and things. I spread them out over the whole desk. He moved his papers all around. He then called:

"Sofie, come here."

When Grandmother came he said:

"Take care of him. You see how he is. Everything's getting out of order."

"Why don't you say that to him," she said. "He's nice and obedient."

"I don't have the heart," he said.

"Come now, Jan," she said. "You shouldn't bother Grandfather."

"He's welcome to stay here if only he doesn't get up on the desk," he said.

Then I looked at the photo and said:

"That's great grandfather and great grandmother."

"Father was 78," he said. "He died in 1911. He was from Myres. Mother would have been 87 when she died. That was 1920. She was born in Gunners. You never met them. They had a hard life. They had to work very hard."

He had taken out the family book. It lay on the desk. He lifted it up out of its case and opened it. He had read to me out of it before. Grandmother used to tell about the people in there.

"Here they are all together," he said. "Generation after generation. Here is my father Peres Petter Ersson. Born 30th September 1833 in Myres. Married 18th November 1858. Died 24th July 1911. There's Grandfather. I never got to meet him. Myr Erik Ersson. Born 20th October 1800. Married 15th April 1831. Died 29th May 1873 of chest sickness, it says here. There is Great-grandfather, Myr Erik Persson. Born 18th November 1755. Married 30th March 1796. Died 7th May 1833 of old age. Lived a praiseworthy life, it says here about him. There is Great-great-grandfather, Petter Jönsson born in Löfåsen 30th

December 1732. He was married 11 October 1752. He moved away from the farm and broke new ground. He died 10 January 1802 of consumption. About him it says he lived modestly. Here is Great-great-great-grandfather, Jöns Danielsson of Löfåsen. He was born in March 1694. He died 31st March 1772. 'Lived innocently,' it says here about him. Who his father was I don't know.

He had folded his hands. He began to sing. First quietly and then more loudly. He had a beautiful voice. He and Grandmother had met in the lodge's choir when they were young people in Gustafs.

Härlig är jorden
Härlig är Guds himmel,
Skön är själarnas pilgrimssång.
Genom de fagra
Riken på jorden
Gå vi till paradis med sång.

Beautiful is Earth
Beautiful is God's Heaven,
Beautiful the pilgrim songs the souls are singing.
Through the beautiful riches on Earth
We go to paradise with song.

Tidevarv komma,
Tidevarv försvinna,
Släkten följa släktens gång.
Aldrig förstummas
Tonen från himlen
I själens glada pilgrimssång.

The ages come,
The ages go,
Generation on generation.
Never stilled the sound from Heaven,
The blessed pilgrim songs of the souls.

At the end of the first verse I noticed that Grandfather had started to weep. While he sang the second verse tears ran down his cheeks and the voice began to break into deep sobs until it was completely overtaken by convulsive shaking. He sat straight up in the chair at the desk with his eyes open and wept soft sobs which seemed to come from deep within the body.

It was then that I knew he would die.

CHAPTER 6

Suddenly I know why the dead sat there the way they did down in the dining room and kitchen the other night. The dead who sat there on their chairs and looked straight ahead. It must have been the same day that Grandfather took out the family book. I sat by the cliff across the road and with a stone tried to hammer my way down into the cliff. I tried hard. I had scraped away the moss. Stone met mountain with a dry hard sound. You could see where it had hit because there the mountain got a white scar. The stone was slowly ground to powder and made my hand sore, but I continued to pound. I wanted to hammer my way down into the cave. The mountain into which I as a six-year-old tried to pound my way doesn't exist. We drive by Gesta from time to time. We take a detour through Stallarholm to Strängnäs and then we drive by the farm. It happens maybe every other year. I have never stopped. I have never gone over the field toward the house. I assume the present occupants would let me in. People are usually friendly when someone wants to see his childhood home. But we have never stopped. When we drive by Gesta I can see the mountain in the woods if I turn away from the big white house to the left, look out to the right instead. It should be there on the other side of the road. But the mountain is no mountain and the woods no woods. It is a ledge in the slope where grain and pine trees grow.

But then it was a mountain and in the mountain there was a cave and if you lowered yourself through the rock you could come down into the hall and there were treasures. I had heard various stories about mountain kings and about the small peo-

ple and about the lady of the mountain and about piles of
stones lifted on pillars of fire, about knights and about all hidden treasure. By this time I must have read them as well. But
the cave here under the mountain was no tale. This cave existed. I think it was Harry who first told me about it. He lived on
the farm and he played with me. He was a little older and had
been asked to look out for me. But now I sat alone here and
beat with stones against the rock covering the cave.

Now I could see down into the cave. Even Great-grandfather and Great-grandmother sat there on their chairs against the
wall as they did in the torn and yellowed photograph
Grandfather held out. They looked straight ahead and sat completely still in the darkness. They were serious. They sat side by
side. She sat with her hands on her knees. The hands were
rough. She had two gold rings on her left hand ring finger. She
sat so she showed them in the darkness. Her dress was black.
It was buttoned up to the neck with twelve buttons. The thir-
teenth was a brooch. He was broad shouldered and held his
right arm behind her. The left hand was in a fist. It rested
against the knee. I saw them down there when I pounded. I
saw them very clearly.

Down in the yard Grandfather came out of his office. He
looked up at the clouds. There was a wind in the air. Maybe
there would be rain. He stood still a moment. A large man with
a pointed beard and a big stomach. Then he continued toward
the field. He was sick now and for food he could only suck raw
eggs, but he didn't want that to show when he walked. His portrait hangs in what used to be the children's room but now is a
guest room. The children still stay overnight there when they
come by. The grandchildren too. A large photograph in an oval
frame. Grandfather and Grandmother. Carl Adolf Pettersson and
Anna Sofia Pettersson born Karlsson. He and I are almost the

same age now. I am 55 and he is 57 when he goes out of the office and away toward the yard in the summer of 1933.

But we are not only getting to be the same age. In the morning when I go down to work it is still night. They told me that when I was a child I got up about five o'clock. When I was a little older I lay and lingered in bed. When I was with Grandfather he was always up many hours before I awoke. Now I get up so I can listen to the news from London at five o'clock while I drink coffee. Not even the dog bothers to get up. Only the cat greets me when I come into the kitchen. Then he goes out. There are two, sometimes three, hours before the house awakens. On the way to my workroom I pass the large glass windows facing out toward the lake. They go from the floor to the ceiling. I don't turn on any lights until I come to the workroom. In the dark glass against the night I meet myself coming. A crude man with a big stomach wearing knicker-bockers and green knit knee socks. Here in the country I go in knickerbockers most of the time from autumn until spring. It is most comfortable that way. I walk a lot in the woods. I change clothes when I go into Stockholm. It is difficult now to say whether the one I meet in the darkness is him or me.

We are about equally stout. At one time he was really fat. That was during the First World War when he was in business, and business was done in the tavern. Now the last few decades he had been heavy and large-stomached like me without being actually fat or flabby.

It wasn't until the later years I saw him that way. It was when I had become 50 that I understood we were getting to be the same age.

CHAPTER 7

That autumn I went to Olaf's School. It must have been when
I began the first grade. It was a private experimental school
where Stockholm's radical intelligentsia sent their children to
freely develop their personalities in cooperation between the
parents and teachers. That sounded ominous.

I could read. When and how I learned I don't know. I could
also write in a manner of speaking. I had started to draw letters
several years earlier. When I look through old papers, I see that
I wrote words the year before. Words with meaning. But the
first attempt to use letters to put stories together comes in the
fall of 1933 and then on a typewriter. My letters were hopeless-
ly messy. Most of the time I wrote in mirror script. During two
years in Olof's School I developed my personality in the alpha-
bet and handwriting. After that no one, not in school or later in
life, could read what I wrote by hand. No one except me. I can
read my notes. Now that has advantages. I make a lot of notes
on trips. I fill one book after the other. But police and customs
agents and others who open bags and snoop through papers
and leaf through notebooks can read nothing. Not a word.
When someone says it looks like a strange cuneiform or rows
of stick men, I don't know. I can read it. I made it myself. But
Gun can't read what I've written by hand, even though she has
tried through more than a quarter of a century and my children
can't read anything either if I've written without a typewriter at
hand. I freely developed a personal handwriting.

I was dyslexic too. I reversed letters and had difficulty with
double consonants. Gradually that also became a problem.
Now I compensate by using a spelling list. I have done that

since I began at *Värmlands Folkblad* as a volunteer in the fall
of 1944. Now I have eyeglasses too. But then in Olof's School
and later during childhood the letters skipped when I tried to
look at them. It was especially difficult when there were several Ms or Ns together. It was difficult to count the strokes when
the letters were small. Numbers were a little different. Certainly
it was never possible to see if there were four or five or maybe
six zeros in a row, and they rolled in and out of each other. But
they were larger and rounder and could be held fast when I
added them one after the other. It was when the paper lay on
the table that it was most difficult. Then all the letters jumped
around. When I brought it closer to me and looked at it with the
other eye it went fine. But I was told that was an ugly habit and
I would destroy my eyesight. But I did it anyway when they
didn't have their eyes on me. So that was how I read.

When I was twelve years old and able to take care of myself
I went to the eye doctor and got glasses. Then it got better. My
mother who studied psychology had observed me and noted
behavioral disturbances.

Note: mirror script.

Fine motor skills disturbed.

But I did not get the glasses until I took care of it myself six
years later.

Now I was going to the first grade and the letters jumped
around if I didn't hold them down. But I was used to that.
School was on Valhallavägen. It was in an ordinary building,
though I remember also that we had classes in an old artillery
regiment's armory at Storgatan. I can't place the memory in
time. We took hikes in Lill-Jans Forest. The leaves were red and
gold. I had a knife. You could make the knife sharper by stick-
ing it down into the sand, Gabriel said. We loitered on a hillside
behind the bushes so the teacher wouldn't see us and take

away our knives, and we stuck them into the ground time after time. But I didn't think my knife got any sharper. Maybe it even got a little duller. It smelled of rain and autumn. After I dried off the knife blade and stuck it back in the sheath on my belt and snapped it down, we ran down the slope toward the other children. We jumped through the leaves. When the sun went behind the clouds the landscape's colors all changed in front of us. The teacher called.

It was in craft class. I stood at the window and looked out. The window was so deep I could have my whole arm on the window sill and still only brush the glass. It rained and the sky was dark. It blew and the trees' cold branches moved in front of the window. It was as if they were trying to scratch their way in. I didn't know what I should do. I just heard the blowing out there and so had all the children in the class.

Then the craft teacher came. He had blond hair and his hair parted in the middle and knickers.

"What are you doing there?" he said.

"I'm unemployed," I said.

"Unemployed? You don't know what unemployment is, you and your kind. There are 200,000 unemployed and a snotty kid from an upper class Social Democratic home says that he is unemployed when he's being lazy."

He was red in the face and angry.

"Here one has to put up with social democracy's offspring all day long," he said.

I didn't answer . There was nothing to say. He talked about professors and Social Democrats, so I began to build a box. I hammered a nail. First a soft hit then a soft hit and then a real hit. Then again a soft hit and a soft hit and a real hit. Suddenly the craft teacher was standing in front of me again. I pretended not to see him. He was not there. I continued to hammer.

"Stop that," he said.

"What?" I said.

"Don't play with the tools," he said. "Don't stand there playing with the hammer."

"I'm not playing," I said.

"Hammer properly," he said.

"Grandfather taught me," I said. "First you aim and then you hit. And he was a building contractor."

Then the crafts teacher became very angry again.

"A builder?" he said. "A builder? He was a cheat. Don't you think I know who he was. His shacks fell down even before they were finished. It was on the South Side. Nice Social Democrat."

"He's not a Social Democrat," I said. "He is a conservative."

"No," said the crafts teacher. "I will tell you who your Grandfather is. He is a robber capitalist. He is a goulash baron, the kind who becomes fat on the sweat of others. He is a war profiteer. He took his profits and turned himself into a landowner. Someone like that should be hung. Such people are parasites. In Germany they've rid themselves of that mob."

The crafts teacher stood with his feet apart in front of me and spoke so loudly that I felt myself getting red in the face. Then he turned on his heels and left the room. Gabriel came up to me and whispered:

"He is a Lindholm follower, a Nazi."

When the crafts teacher came back he didn't look in my direction. I continued to pound in the nails. I hit first a light hit and then a light hit and then a hard one and then a real hit and I built my box. The box was going to have different drawers and in one drawer I would put the craft teacher's heart, which I would cut out with my knife. In another drawer I would put his two ears and in a big drawer I would put his hands. But I don't tell anyone about this. Not even Gabriel.

CHAPTER 8

I am six years old. It is autumn and every day I go to school. I eat oatmeal with milk. While I sit at the kitchen table and eat breakfast I look out over the canal and away toward the palace. The mornings are getting dark. The leaves have fallen. Soon the street lights are on when I come into the kitchen. Mary still has to help me with my shoelaces sometimes. It is difficult to thread them so you only need one pull to tighten them. I go out the door and down the steps and then I don't remember. I want to say I have two images and they don't fit together. I am not sure how I get from home in Kungsholmen to school on the other side of the city, near Karlaplan. I write "near Karlaplan" or "in the Karlaplan neighborhood" because here too my memories get mixed up and show at once a school high up in a building on Valhallavägen and in the old armory at Storgatan. The images are very clear. In one image I can open a tall white door and come out in a corridor. The white paint on the door panel is peeling. It is Valhallavägen. There is also a large window. We have made a flying machine of paper boxes and got a little boy, a boy who is smaller than the rest of us, and therefore is willing to allow himself to be put in the box. We are pushing the flying machine out through the window so he can fly away toward Gärdet when the teacher comes in the door. She screams. We are on the fifth floor. She picks up the boy and destroys our flying machine. Gabriel says:

"Maybe he was too heavy."

In the other image we have gone into the armory's shed. There are bales of pressed hay. We climb among the bales. A few other boys have made a passage through the bales. There is something like a cave in the hay. Far inside they have a hiding place. There they sit and smoke sometimes. From inside there no smell can get out and betray them. They are careful with the fire. They lay there and read newspapers with pictures of girls. After a while they kick us out.

"Out with you."

Some of the images of how I get to school I can't see clearly. On the other hand, there are two images of me on the way from school to Kungsholmstrand. In one I have just climbed out of the streetcar on St. Eriksgatan and walked down the steps to the chocolate factory and am now on my way through the gate. In the other I ride the bus. Number 66, I think. The conductor knows who I am because I often ride that same bus and he talks to me.

Mary still lets me stay home sick when *Allers* comes. She helps me with cutouts too. I think it was that autumn *Allers* had the steamroller. There was a street and on the street was a steamroller to cut out. There was a man too. He was partly an ordinary man who stood up and partly something which had been completely flattened. You clipped him out and fit him into two slots on the street. When you put everything together you could drive the steamroller over the street toward the man and run over him and leave him like a big flat spot on the road. You only needed to pull in one flap and the man was completely run over.

In the evenings when Mary is free and the parents don't have guests or something her fiancé comes. He is going to be a pastor. Sometimes he takes me along when he goes for a walk. We go up St. Eriksgatan and then we go down Fleminggatan until we come to the city. That begins at Kungsbron and the market place and the railroad tracks to the central station. We go along Kungsgatan and Mary and her fiancé look in the shop windows and talk. When we come to Hötorget it is already so dark that we can see neon lights.

When we are on the way home we begin to talk about Grandfather.

"He has given me presents worth a million crowns," I say.

"Don't talk nonsense," says Mary.

"But he is a millionaire," I say.

"Not any more, anyway," says Mary's fiancé.

It is completely dark when we go up Fleminggatan and Mary and her fiancé talk to each other the whole time.

In the evenings before night comes, I build. It is possible to build a whole city. Buildings with streets and bridges and railroads. But when I have finished building for the evening and am ready to take my clothes off and wash myself and go to bed I am careful to make a large free path through the room toward the door. Because when the night comes and it is quiet and everyone sleeps I have to run.

They don't like me to run. Alva comes into the room and questions me. She turns on the ceiling light when she comes in. She sits on the edge of the bed and tries to talk to me. She is blonde. She asks questions and more questions. She reaches for me and I pull back. Her fingertips are very cold. It makes me shiver when she touches me. I freeze from her and say:

"It is like a big mountain with snow on it."

"What?" she says.

"A completely dark sky with high mountains with snow on them and it is a long way from one mountain to the next. A person is standing on every mountain and you can see the people because there is snow and snow is white. Stars twinkle in the snow. This way you can see that people are standing up on the mountains."

"Poor little one," she says.

I understand that it is wrong to tell her anything. She cannot see. She reaches for me again and I draw away from her in the bed. I see the mountain very clearly even though the ceiling light is on. Now fifty years later I think I know which mountains I was looking at. I think they are Hans Christian Andersen's Swiss Alps which I made larger and more lonely. Now the clouds go behind the mountain and make huge cold figures and Alva leans forward and questions and questions. But I have pulled myself away and see the mountains right through her and high up there in the dark comes a big bird with spread wings. It is probably an eagle. The stars twinkle around the eagle. Now Gunnar calls to Alva that the guests are already at the door. She goes and it is quiet in the room and I let the eagles sweep past close to me so I can feel the draft against my cheeks.

Later I take the eagles away and think about cars. In the toy store on St. Eriksgatan on the other side of the bridge there is a car I would want to buy if I had the money. I often go across the bridge to look at it. It is there in the show window. It is a big fire truck. It is not made of sheet metal. It is cast iron. I have picked it up. It is red. It is very big and has a yellow ladder you can crank up. I would like to have that car and take it out and drive it and crank up the ladder and let the firefighters climb up. They climb and climb and there are more and more of them and now all the pictures go away and I sleep.

CHAPTER 9

I am at home at Gesta and Grandfather is sick. He lies on his bed. Out there it blows in the trees and I lie on the floor in his room and read the Book of Inventions. I like the pictures which show ocean steamers in cross section and what it looks like in Paris when you take up the street and expose the subway and sewers and water mains. I like to read about machines. It is exciting.

"You will probably be an engineer," says Grandfather.

"I'm going to be an inventor," I say. "I'm going to invent steam engines that can go whole days with almost no fuel."

Grandmother is concerned that I will make Grandfather tired. But he says:

"Let the boy stay here with me a little bit."

I continue to read in the *Book of Inventions* and Grandfather says:

"I used to like to sing when I was a child. They always used to say I was musical and thought I could be a cantor. I dreamed of that. In 1896 I came to Stockholm with Janne Eriksson from Stora Skedvi. We worked at Stora Kopparbergs' exhibit for the big Stockholm exhibition which opened in May 1897 on Lejonsslätten at Djurgårdsbrunnsviken. I took a day off and dressed up and went to the music academy on Blasieholmen and knocked on the door and asked to enroll in the conservatory's church choir program. I was so naive I thought you only needed to knock. I had only had elementary school and was a carpenter at the exhibition ground. They laughed out loud at me."

When I go home from Gesta to Stockholm again it is not

Grandfather who drives. But I don't remember the driver's name. I think it was the chauffeur. He drove me to Läggesta and there I was put on the train for Stockholm. It was the last time I saw Grandfather.

Around Lucia Day a girl was killed as she went sliding. It was on the slide near Valhallavägen. One morning when we were going sliding there was a big red blotch on the ice. The children saw that a girl had tumbled.

"She hit her head so hard it was smashed."

"Her name was Inga and she died."

The children didn't want to go sliding over the red. They started further down. But then the slide became very short. You couldn't get up any speed either. I ran to get a real take off and slid over the red and beyond and after me followed Gabriel and the red went deep down into the ice and when we slid over it with our boots we yelled:

"Now we are grinding away Inga's brain!"

After a while the other children followed.

At Christmas there was going to be a big assembly before vacation. The various classes were to demonstrate various things. But I didn't want to do what the class did. I wanted to do something on my own. I wanted to read something. I got to do what I wanted. The whole room was full of children and older students and parents and teachers. I had taken along volume two of the *Book of Inventions*, the volume that had to do with various natural resources and how they could be used. I had decided to read about the steam engine. I read well. Of everyone I knew, I was the best at reading aloud. I thought the steam engine was an important thing to read about.

"One could say without exaggeration that the steam engine is the present day's most necessary power machine. Yes, all of modern industry is essentially based on this invention and its application. It has also had an incalculable influence on the whole of industrial development during the past century. But with steam power's help the earth's hidden treasures are taken up and changed after melting down and all kinds of processing into the most diverse forms for the most varied uses."

Now the whole room had begun to giggle and make noise and clear throats and move around. But I continued anyway and tried to raise my voice to speak over the giggling.

"This power makes possible, among other things, materials for our steam vehicles and railroads and helps us to build these means of transportation and in the end puts life in the dead machines."

People laughed out loud and applauded and forced me to be quiet and I looked up at them and imagined they were no longer there. They were gone and the room was empty. I had done away with them, closed the book and put it on my head and balanced it there while I imagined them gone.

After a while the teacher came and led me out. The performance continued with the children performing a play.

That Christmas I got *Texas Jack*. I began to read it when the evening was over and I was left alone. I lay in my bed with the lamp on and read. I remember that he rescued a noble family at a hacienda which rebels were going to burn. He raced against the fire. I had made my way through one chapter and come a good bit into the second when Alva suddenly opened the door. She had caught me. She had probably seen the light in the cracks of the door.

"My God, the boy is awake," she cried.

CHAPTER 10

When Grandfather died, they went home to Gesta and left me in Stockholm. The telephone rang with the news and then they packed and ran back and forth through the apartment and then they departed. I didn't get to go along. It wasn't fitting. It was January 1934. I didn't get to go to Grandfather's burial either.

The evening he died I sat in the darkness in the dining room without turning on any lamps and looked out over Kungsholmstrand. The apartment was dark and cold behind me. But that didn't mean anything. I heard Mary in the kitchen. She thought I was in my room. She fixed food for me. I heard her go to my room to get me. Then she came to the dining room.

"Are you sitting here in the darkness?" she said.

There was black sausage with lingonberries. When I had eaten I talked to her, but I don't remember about what.

In the night later a dream came which I continued to dream for the next few years. Sometimes I wonder if I can still dream it. It tingles in my legs and back and raises the hair on my arms when I write it and still it is so literary and narrative that I can't really understand where I got the details.

I come walking toward a church in the country and it is not Toresund, but it is an ordinary white church with a black roof and tower. The path is gravel. To the left are burial chapels. They stand in a row side by side. One could say that each chapel is like a hood of earth. There are iron gates and large black doors. The doors are open. There is a girl from Dalecarlia in the door. She is very pretty and blonde and smiles at me.

Behind her a stairway leads down into the darkness. She invites me to come in. What happens next I don't know, but I'm chilled. Strangely enough, I am chilled even now when I write this. I don't tell anyone about the Dalecarlia girl dream. There are strangely ornate wrought iron bars.

I know the dream came for the first time the night Grandfather died. I know that because I always thought of that when I had that dream as a child. I don't know if I became really afraid. It was a different dream. It didn't make me run, I just froze.

When I take down the dream picture and look at it I can't place it. I didn't know many churches. This church with the burial chapels and flat country was unfamiliar. When I look more closely at the burial chapel I see it is baroque architecture. Ornate and swelling and with a gaping vault. The image and various details must have come from some book. But I can't remember that we had any books about old architecture. We had many books about "funkis," functional design. German picture books with newly built white houses and various plans and Swedish picture books from the Stockholm exhibition and French picture books with houses. But no books with pictures of old houses. But wherever the image of the old burial chapel came from, there are pictures of old architecture. Maybe it was a chapel I had seen as a child in Germany or France.

The girl from Dalecarlia was not in costume. She always went around dressed like that. But who she was I didn't know. I had a fairy tale figure I liked a lot. Her name was Stella and she was in a book. She disappeared toward the end of the book and was found among the stars. I occasionally stood at the window in my room in the evening and looked up out of the garden toward the sky and saw stars. I thought of Stella and let a strange sweet cry come up out of my body and I started to cry

out loud. Alva came upon me once. It became an ice cold
shame. She came into the room and she reached for me and I
thought, "Now she's going to say it." And she said it.

"Poor little one. What need for affection you have."

The shame was an icicle, straight from the neck through the
body, out the feet and I hoped she would go far far away. But
she took out her black notebook and made notes.

There was something about the Dalecarlia girl that was like
Stella. But she was different also and I don't know where she
came from. For the most part, I usually know where the images
come from. But this one was a strange dream. A dream in costume, I might say.

They took me along to the auction. Everything was being
sold. It was summer. I went through the rooms. People were
noisy and happy. I watched while the gavel came down and
things disappeared. I had 25 öre. I bid for two ceramic stoves
and as no one else wanted to have them, I got them. They were
fine ceramic stoves from the room on the first floor. When I said
I had bought the ceramic stoves Gunnar got angry. He talked to
the auctioneer, who threw up his hands and said it was not
such a big problem. I got back my 25 öre and even the ceramic stoves were destroyed.

The house was now very large and empty. It was full of
refuse. In Grandfather's office there was no furniture left. In the
corner under the window there was a little white paper. I
turned it over. It was a business card.

"C.A. Pettersson. Landowner. Telephone: Stallarholmen 17.
Gesta Gård. Address: Malmby."

That was all that was left. In the yard they sat and ate now
that the auction was over. I looked at them through the window. They had run around and hunted for me and called me,
but had not found me because I could hide myself at Gesta.

They ate pork chops with spinach in white sauce. They drank soft drinks. Everything had come to an end.

I don't have much from Gesta. When Grandmother finally moved to Stockholm because she had become too old to take care of herself I got a few pieces of white garden furniture and a sofa. The garden furniture was made in the Gesta furniture shop and if I had not taken it, it would have burned up. The sofa was old and worthless. It had been made by a carpenter at the turn of the century. It was the one which had been in the upper hall. I used to lie on it and fantasize. I used to call it the jungle sofa. It had heavy upholstery with plant patterns. Now it is in Gun's studio and we use it as an extra bed for guests.

But I didn't inherit anything from home when Grandmother died. Gunnar didn't want me to. He deliberately gave away his whole share so that I would get nothing. My aunt Elsa was upset about that. She and Uncle Gösta discussed it and talked with their children, my cousins. Then I got two copper pans they had bought at the auction in 1934.

"You should have something of Mother's," said Elsa. "It's not right of Gunnar to try to see that nothing from home at Gesta goes to you. To your Grandfather and Grandmother you were just like their own child, a late born child. Gesta was your childhood home."

I was in Kabul when I heard that Grandmother had died. It was 1965. She was 87. In the night she had got up and said:

"Now I'm going home." Then she walked out the window. She lived a few hours in the hospital where they took her in an ambulance after she had fallen down among the bushes in the yard. She never regained consciousness. There had to be a police inquiry, but it was regarded as an accident. Senility. But I don't know if that was so. She was old and she could just have got tired of everything too.

"I am so sad," she used to say at the end. "It is so difficult, everything. I wanted the family to stay together."

She was not so confused that she didn't know what she wanted.

I have what she then wrote me to read when I was older about the days when I grew up with her and Grandfather at Gesta. It was among the papers and it wasn't until the seventies that I opened the package. I began to read towards the end of the book.

"One Sunday afternoon your Grandfather was supposed to go to Stallarholm dairy." (In the corner is written in another ink, "that was in July 1930.") "And he asked us to go along. We two sat in the back of the car. When we got about half the way you said in a dissatisfied tone:

"'This is not Jan's road.'

"When we got out we went out on the bridge and you got on your knees and looked down into the water. Then the dairyman's wife came out and asked us to come in. She wanted to offer us coffee. You and I went inside with her. We were alone a while in a room with a boy ten or eleven years old. He sat quietly with a book in his hand.

"You and I sat on the sofa.

"Then you said:

"'Grandma, the boy is ugly.'

"I was quiet. After a while you said:

"'Grandma, the boy is stupid, too.'

"Then we were invited in to coffee in another room and Grandfather also. But not you. Oh no. No coffee in Grandma's company.

"'What will the boy have?' asked Mrs. P.

"'He usually gets milk,' I said.

"But you didn't want anything. You came and sat in my lap

while I drank coffee. But you did not take a single taste of even one cake. You said to me:

"'Jan can leave those cakes alone, he can.'

"Then we went home. Then you wanted to eat, and you did, too. Then you said:

"'Now Jan is glad to be in his own home.'

"When we went out, you were always glad when you came home. You liked best to be at home. When we came to Aunt Rut, you could say:

"'Now we're going home to Gesta.'

"Yes, dear Jan, this book did not become what I expected it to be. But that can't be helped. Now the years have gone, and big changes have happened. I am now alone at Mariefred. As you know, Grandfather died Sunday, the 21st of January at 4:15 in the afternoon. Then we sold Gesta, the 29th of June 1934. I moved here to Mariefred."

When I read that it was suddenly the spring of 1934 again in the middle of the fall. I stand in Grandfather's empty office at home at Gesta and I am seven and hold his business card in my hand and look out through the window over the yard and fields and it is all over and I begin to sniff and sit like a big fat 50-year-old at my work table and cry until I'm trembling.

CHAPTER 11

I wondered about my origins and who my parents really were and about my birth. Alva and Gunnar were taking care of me now but I didn't believe they were my real parents. Maybe I was a foundling or a bastard who had been adopted.

There is nothing unusual about such speculations. Almost all children in our culture have them. You don't understand what you are doing in that family. You don't understand how such strange people can be your parents. You wonder if you aren't really someone else. It usually passes with time. In the end the speculations are forgotten and you begin to speak of your childhood as if it had been pleasant. In my case it wasn't forgotten. It became clearer as the years went by. It was not a matter of speculations and normal childhood misconceptions. There was a difference between how my friends and their parents behaved with each other, and how Alva and Gunnar behaved with me and how I felt about them. Later when my sisters were born I noticed that my parents were not so different from my friends' parents. That wasn't the reason the atmosphere was so strange with me. They behaved toward my sisters about the same as my friends' parents did with their children. But with me it was different. I thought about that a lot.

I noticed that all my relatives used to say I had come straight from heaven. No one knew I was going to be born. Alva hadn't told anyone she was going to have a child before they heard I was born twenty minutes after four on the afternoon of July 19, 1927, a Tuesday. I weighed 7 pounds 1 ounce and was 19 1/2 inches tall. I used to doubt that Alva was my mother. Now I am almost inclined to believe she actually is my mother. But I am still not convinced.

The family tree and family relationships have a social meaning. I can say my father's-father's-mother's-father's-father's-father's-father's-father's-father's-father was called Erik Svenson and died in 1688. Or I can say Eloise is my second cousin. It is true in the social sense even if it no longer is socially relevant. Families dissolve and siblings can beat each other to death and "sisters' children break kinship" without that leading to any twilight of the gods and end of the world. But if I thought that statement was also true in a biological sense I would have gone a long way out into the quagmire. About 14 percent of all children with blood types on file with the health department have a different blood group than is possible if the person officially registered as their father, and who they believe to be their father, really is their father. It takes a wise man to recognize his true blood relatives.

But if paternity is uncertain, maternity is no less doubtful. I was present when my daughter was born in Paris, so I am certain she was born. Afterward I got a paper: child, sex feminine. With that, I was to go to the authorities. If I had wanted to, I could have written "mother unknown." That is the Napoleonic Code. I didn't do that. But I could have done that. In Sweden that would not work. But just as I know that people have gone to prison for each other, I know that people have borne children for each other. It is no more remarkable to go to a hospital in another's name than it is to go through the judicial system under another name. Before personal identity numbers and data followed us through life, it was even easier.

I had no proof that it was Alva who was my natural mother. But I find it plausible. Mostly because I never could understand what the motive would be for mystification. I remember that I asked Gunnar about it one Sunday dinner.

"Am I your illegitimate son?"

He only got angry. He didn't answer, but left the table and slammed the door behind him. I must have been about ten years old. In any case, my sisters were already born.

It was about that time I read in Alva's books that such thoughts are common among children. They suggested one thing or another. Because I knew everything suggested something else, I was careful when I talked with them. You had to choose your words so you were not understood. For the most part it was not a matter of saying something totally different from what I felt, and making them try to figure it out. Most often I felt just what I said. I learned to be vigilant and careful with my words.

What I thought about then as a ten-year old, when I read that it was common for children to puzzle over their origins and believe that there was some secret about their birth, was that it could very well be true I was just like the other children in this respect. But out of all those who believed there was something strange about their origins, there must be a few (a small few, but still a few) who in fact had strange origins. How could I know I wasn't one of those?

But I didn't think I wasn't in some way related to Alva and Gunnar. We were related; I just couldn't understand how. Gunnar too had recessive ear lobes. That was a sign of a born criminal, it said in one of Alva's books. The one about Lombroso and other things that had pictures of various signs of criminality. But we were so very different too. With animals, for example.

I always wanted to have animals. I had had them at Gesta. In the summers when I was at Kvicksta I spent a lot of time with the dogs. I've always gotten along well with animals. I feel inside me what they want. It's like that with children. It doesn't take any special interest to be able to take care of children or animals. You just do it. But Alva saw this interest in animals as a sign of emotional disturbance. She had read about children who were disturbed and wanted to be around animals. That is why it was not until I was twelve, almost thirteen, that I was able to nag them into letting me have pets. Then I got a dachshund.

By that time I had begun to realize that I wasn't the one with the problem. Whether she ever understood that, I don't know. I don't think so. In the early sixties when I came home to Sweden and we spent some time together, I was up at Västerlånggatan to talk to her about something. I had my dalmatian with me, a bitch called Cheeta. Alva got nervous.

"She's probably going to wet the floor," she said.

Cheeta had to stay leashed in the bathtub while I was there.

Her inability to relate to animals was almost touching, I thought then. My daughter was going to take care of our cat when we went to Afghanistan in 1965. Alva promised to take the basket with the cat on the train to Göteborg. It was a large tomcat with white paws, a typical Sörmland cat. A good rat-catcher. It hated to be in the basket. It clawed and scratched to get out. When my daughter got the basket with the cat from Alva, she opened the lid carefully. The cat took off across the floor and then leaped up onto the hatrack. It lay there crouching. It swished its tail and made soft angry noises.

"Well, it likes being here, anyway," said Alva. "It's waving its tail and purring." And she was not joking. She was not receptive to their signals. She lacked intuition. Animal behavior was something to read about in a book and she totally misinterpreted the living creatures.

With children it was the same as with animals. She couldn't take care of them and she wasn't capable of reacting spontaneously to their signals. She studied childrearing. When I was five or six years old she taught courses in child psychology and parenting. That seemed to me an example of black and surrealistic humor as soon as I was old enough to reflect on it.

She simply was not good with children. When I was grown and had my own children I saw how awkwardly she touched them. As if her hands didn't really belong to her body. She laughed shrilly and her voice was tense when she tried to talk baby talk with them. The children would look at her and start to scream and get blue in the cheeks. She had cold fingers.

I took baths by myself. Alva gave me good advice. It was important to have a clean bottom and have clean underwear because you might fall under a streetcar and go to the hospital and there they might discover that you hadn't changed your underpants. Her grandmother had said to her:

"No one sees your empty gut, but they all see your ragged undershirt."

It was important to be clean underneath.

At Kungsholmsstrand I didn't shit. I went to the toilet and had a bowel movement and the brown stuff I left after myself was called "feces." It was only repulsive people who slapped each other on the behind. I would never do that. In Säter when Alva once had to help Grandmother knead dough in the kitchen, she said:

"Where do you keep the utensils?"

"Use your hands, Alva dear," said Grandmother. "It's much easier that way."

Perhaps this distaste for bodily functions made Alva keep her pregnancy a secret and that was why the family was surprised when I was born and had suddenly appeared. I am now inclined to believe that she is my biological mother. But she behaved strangely about my birth all her life.

Anyone who looks at the official 1981 biography that according to the introduction had been written by Lars G. Linskog in cooperation with Alva Myrdal and carefully checked by her in manuscript will notice that I was never born. She studies in England and Germany in 1927, works on a Master's thesis, "Critique of Freud's Theory of Dreams," in 1929, but interrupts her work when she gets a Rockefeller fellowship and travels to the U.S.A. in October 1929. My sister Sissela was born according to that biography in the middle of the debate about Alva's and Gunnar's book *The Population Crisis*. But I suspect that Sissela was more a contribution to a debate than a child. I exist in the birth register and in the early church registers. After 1940 I don't appear in any of the official records concerning her. She then has only two daughters. It could be said she did not mention her firstborn out of her concern for privacy. But such reserve goes far beyond what is normal. As a child I didn't have much understanding of her behavior. I didn't feel as if I had been deprived of my right as firstborn, but of my right to official existence.

With Sissela and Kaj it was a little different. As a result, they also developed differently. The strange lack of contact was the same, though. It was noticeable with Kaj. She refused to speak until she was almost four years old. She just grunted and pointed. Gunnar thought that was very funny and an amusing story to tell people and took Kaj out to guests and showed her off. I should probably add that Kaj was a gifted and really sweet kid who liked animals and people. Sissela was the one they liked best. Gunnar called her the "Little Hypocrite" She was proud of being called that. She was the one most like them.

I was lent out starting when I was small. That's how I came to live at Gesta. Later I lived with various relatives. Not once did I spend the summer with Alva and Gunnar. They avoided taking me along after we came home from Switzerland when I was four. As soon as I was seventeen and started to volunteer at *Värmland's Folkblad,* Alva gave away my desk, and all my junk—the newspapers and magazines I had saved—was thrown out and I lost my room. When I came to Bromma later and lived with them I had to live in the air-raid shelter. I furnished it with mattresses and a low table and flower vases with green climbing plants.

But this wouldn't mean much in itself. If children were harmed by separation from their parents for the greater part of their childhoods, then the British upper class and the French bourgeoisie's children would have suffered irreparable harm over two hundred years. Which is obviously not the case. And the children of the Swedish merchant fleet weren't ruined either.

What I felt as a child was not only that they kept me out of the way and didn't want to have anything to do with me, but that they actually disliked me. I was a mistake.

CHAPTER 12

Now the wind is blowing and the telephone wires are singing. The whole world is white and the road is newly plowed. Grandfather took care of that. Along the ditch stand large brooms. A magpie sits on the pole and looks at me. It has laid its head to the side and blinks at me. I stand under the pole and can hear all the talk in the world go through the telephone wires. But it is so much talk that it all becomes a song in the wind. The magpie pays no attention to me. It just blinks.

I plod up the hill where the cows go in the summertime. There is snow in the air and the sky is gray. The junipers are completely still on the slope and over there the forest begins. The spruces drag their branches toward the snowy ground. Right under the two big junipers I make four angels in the snow. I am very precise when I make snow-angels. The snow cover is completely white and almost unbroken. There is only a rabbit track down there and also my own footprints. The four angels fly so near each other that they can touch each other's fingertips. They have wings with small claws. They are almost like bats, but much larger and all white. Carefully I lay myself on my back in the snow, stretch out my arms and make wings in the snow. I get up without making unnecessary tracks and make the next angel. Now two angels are flying under the left bush. I go back in my tracks and make the third angel at the right bush and then I go out in the snow and make the fourth angel. I step carefully back toward the path in my own footprints.

The footprints now go straight up from the road and come

out to the two junipers, precisely in between them. Then they go to the left and then to the right. They become like a column with a beam over it. Over the beam are four angels holding each other with claws in the wingtips. Over them are two black junipers.

It is cold. I stamp to get warmer. I've got snow in my pants and snow under my bootlaces and the cold nips at my toes. I go home past the school. The schoolyard is not shoveled. There is only a path shoveled from the road to the schoolhouse, and another from the schoolhouse to the outhouse. The children are on winter vacation. The flagstones peek out from under the drifts toward the gray sky. The hedges along the path are high and sprawling. Soon they will hide the school. When I get past the hedges I feel the wind. It comes over the hill and the drifts move. Across the field the lights are on at Aunt Rut's. She is my mother's sister. Elon is my mother's brother. He leases the farmland of Gesta from Grandfather. Ulla is my cousin. She is four months older than I am. Their house is up on the hill. The climbing tree we play in in the summer is all the way down at the field. Now it is black and bony and without leaves. If the field was a sea, they would be living on an island.

The wide white fields are a huge ocean. They are on a bay of Lake Mälar. The drifts are waves which have stiffened in the cold and they steam in the wind. The slopes rise up out of the sea. They are islets and rocks and way far away the land lays dark on the horizon. The drifts begin to wash up over the road. They go diagonally across the plowed path. I plod ahead.

Gösta has said that everything here was sea at one time. He is engaged. He will marry Elsa. She is my aunt. They are both elementary school teachers. Now the snow is really coming. It is blowing in the air. It stings my face and scratches. When I come around the big curve and go past the barn and the red house, the manor house is there. The big house is large and white and the roof is black. Through the blowing snow I can see the windows shine. Lights are on in the office and in the kitchen and upstairs on the second floor. The front yard is plowed and sanded, but the snow wanders in over it. Now the blizzard is darkening and the large open fields below begin to fade away into darkness and snow. But the house is lit and inside is warm. I go toward the kitchen door. I stamp the worst off myself at the entry and open the door.

"If the field were an ocean, we'd be living on an island," I say.

"Hurry up and change your socks so you don't catch cold," says Grandmother.

I stand in the living room with forehead against the window glass and look out over the field in the darkness. Sometimes I think there is a glimmer of light far off in the blizzard. It appears to be coming from Ulriksberg and we are a large ship in the night on the ocean. To the south on the other side on this bay of large fields lie Kumla and Ulriksberg anchored at their wooded slopes and farther into the bay Björkeby and Grandmother's Kvicksta. To the east are Vannesta and Stora Eneby off in the darkness. Out past Toresund church are Norrby and Herrestad and Salby and Räfsnäs. Then there is only Hista and you are at Mariefred and the castle. North of the road is Åkerby and Vaxäng by themselves behind a narrow sound between the woods. Then there are the ordinary farms as well. But these are the manor houses sailing in the night.

I hear Edith coming. She puts down a tray and sets the table. It clatters a little. I get up, no longer leaning my forehead against the cold glass. A steamy spot has appeared on the glass where I breathed. I see Edith in the black glass. She sets the table behind me.

"Come now, Jan," she says.

There is warm milk with sugar and a cinnamon roll to go with it.

"Thank you, Edith," I say.

"Drink now so you get warm," she says.

I swing my legs as I drink the milk. I don't reach all the way down. Tipp is under the table. Tipp is old now and snores. Now and then he breaks wind.

"Tipp let one," I whisper so no one can hear me.

I slide on my chair to reach out my foot and pet him.

"Quiet, Tipp," I say.

He sniffles and wakes. He doesn't even bother to get up. He shuffles himself out of my reach. Then he falls asleep again. He sniffles and snores and breaks wind. Someone must have given him bones again. Now he begins to dream. He jerks in his sleep and tries to bark but he can only moan and growl. I wonder what he's dreaming. Maybe he's dreaming it's summer and we're running and I throw a stick for him. For a while I consider crawling under the table to wake him. He gets such a confused expression in his eyes if you wake him when he's sleeping. It takes a little while before he really knows where he is. But it is probably not nice to wake him that way. He is old now and has a stiff back which makes it hard for him to go down the stairs. I have seen him slide down sometimes. His backbone doesn't support him and he sits and crouches. But I haven't told anyone about that and try to help him down without anyone seeing because they shoot old dogs. Tipp really is too old.

"Poor old Tipp," says Grandfather.

Tipp has not been out in the woods with the hunters for a few years now. We have a horse like that too. One who is too old for anything, but who gets to stay around anyway.

When we eat supper Grandfather is not at home. He is at a meeting. Grandmother and I eat alone. Later she reads and I am busy with my cars. In the night I wake up when the door slams. It is Mela who has come home from Stockholm. She is my aunt. It is almost midnight. She is happy. She opens the door and looks in. When she sees I'm awake, she says:

"Shall I sing the umbrella song?"

She goes out into the hall and gets an umbrella. She opens it up. She sits on the edge of my bed and sits on the edge of my bed and sings about Little Jon Blund with the umbrella. It is funny. Then I must have fallen asleep right away because I don't remember her leaving.

CHAPTER 13

In 1927 Gunnar and Alva had an apartment on Atlasgatan in Stockholm. Many of the younger academics and radical intellectuals lived on Atlas then. It was near the university and was a newly built and well planned neighborhood. Now it is very shabby. All the businesses have closed. Gun and I lived in a two-room apartment on Vulcanusgatan two blocks away in the mid-fifties. We still have a small overnight flat in the building.

I first came to Gesta when I was two weeks old. I was christened at Gesta when I was three weeks old. Grandfather called the family together. Great-grandmother and Great-grandfather came down from Solvarbo. Great-grandfather would die a short time later. Grandfather and Grandmother, aunts and uncles and Uncle Robert. Grandfather had called on the pastor from Toresund church and I was christened in the living room at Gesta. Afterward they drank coffee in the yard. The men were dressed in tails and white bowties. Except Uncle Stig, who was only ten years old. However, he had just had a haircut and combed his hair with water and wore a tie and jacket.

Alva and Gunnar used to leave me at Gesta. Grandmother took care of me. When I was one year and ten months old, Alva arrived on the noon train to Läggesta to drop me off. Grandfather picked me up with the car. It was May 18, 1929. A few weeks later Gunnar and Alva were in London and then traveled to America. On May 13, 1930, the newspaper said that Gunnar had been appointed professor in Geneva. Grandmother showed me the picture. On June 26 that year Gunnar and Alva came from America to take me to Switzerland. Gunnar had bought a car in America and drove down through Sweden and Denmark and Germany and France with Alva and me and Aunt Mela, who had come along to take care of me. In the fall of 1931 Gunnar and Alva were back in Stockholm. Then they got an apartment on Kungsholmsstrand. They became Social Democrats and got their start in politics, but I was at Gesta most of the time. Right after that Gunnar was appointed professor at Stockholm.

Until Grandfather died and Gesta was sold and there was the auction and Grandmother moved to Mariefred the year I was seven years old, Gesta was home and security and taken for granted. Grandmother had taken care of me. She continued to do that. When I could not be placed with some other relative, Grandmother took care of me. Even during the war when Alva and Gunnar traveled to America, Grandmother came to take care of everything. I was already big then, fourteen years old, but my sisters were small. Then hadn't even begun school yet. Grandmother was 63 years old then so it was hard for her with three children and a large house. I probably didn't think about that. It was wartime, too. We all worked hard, and there was lots to do. She got me to take care of the furnace. It was heated with coal and she woke me up early every morning to go down to the cellar to rake and light the fire.

I remember nothing of those first years at Gesta, of course. Or, more correctly said, the memories I think I have are those Grandmother created for me. For years afterward she constantly returned to what I was like during my first years when she had to take care of me. On the other hand, I remember a lot from when I was five and six. In the sixties, when she was way over eighty and I was almost forty, she would still tell me:

"When we were in Strängnäs and went to the pastry shop the waitress said to you, 'Whose boy are you, then?' and you answered, 'I'm Grandma's Jan.' Do you remember that? And you answered 'I'm Grandma's Jan.' Do you remember?"

"Yes, I remember," I said.

"And when your Grandfather asked who you were you said, 'I'm Grandma's little darling.' Do you remember?"

"Yes," I said.

If we weren't alone I used to tell her to be quiet and if she started to cry, she was beginning to be easily moved, I told her to stop. I think I was the only one who could tell her that without getting her upset.

The older I grew the more she talked about my first years. How sweet I was. How smart I was. And how nice I was.

"You were a great joy for all of us and we thought so much of you. One time when you were two years old you said suddenly at the dinner table, 'Jan eat up to roof so Grandma afraid and Grandpa afraid and Mela afraid.' And at first we all thought about what you could mean, but finally we understood and then you were delighted. You meant that you would eat so much you would reach the ceiling and then we'd all be afraid of you.

"You were always so full of life. When you were two and a half we left you alone once in the upstairs hall. I had closed the gate to the stairway, of course. But there was a coffee tray on the table. When I came back you came toward me and looked so self-satisfied. 'Jan did something for Grandma,' you said. I wondered what it was and then I saw what you had done. The cream pitcher was half full of cream and you had filled it the rest of the way with sugar. All the sugar cubes left from the sugar bowl you had put in a row on the tray. You don't remember that."

"Don't cry, Grandmother," I said.

"And then at Christmas 1929 you were alone in the living

room a few minutes and it was very quiet, so I must have become suspicious, but I sat and sewed and then Lilly, the kitchen maid, came calling, 'Ma'am, Ma'am. Jan has taken apart all the chairs in the living room.' She didn't know the chairs came apart. The seats could be lifted out. But you knew. When I came into the living room you sat there on the sofa, you little rascal, with such a satisfied look and all eight seats around on the floor. 'The sofa's not broken,' you said. You were so happy the sofa wasn't broken. We put the seats back together and you promised never to do it again. And you never did.

"Maybe I didn't always do the right thing," she said. "It's not easy to take care of a small child. But I did the best I could."

"Grandma, don't cry," I said.

"No," she said. "I won't. But I had to take care of you. I don't know if I always did the right thing. I worry about that a lot now, but I acted according to my own convictions. You maybe would say I did wrong and was unfair to you."

"Now be quiet, Grandma," I said.

"We had our biggest fight over half a ginger snap. And that was when you were almost three years old. We had been out walking for a while and you and I had talked and had such a nice time. When we came in lunch was ready and I took off all your outer clothes and then you ran, without asking, straight to the sideboard and took a brown ginger snap. It was probably not a big thing, but you shouldn't have done it right before a meal. I fixed a plate of food for you. You saw that and threw half the ginger snap on the floor. I said, 'Pick up the cookie, now, Jan. Then you'll get some good food.' And you answered, 'No, Jan can't do that.' 'You certainly can,' I said. 'No,' you said. 'Jan can't do that.' I asked you several times and got the same answer every time. You were not angry, and neither was I. Then I said, 'I can help you.' I put you on the floor and with my help you held your hand over the cookie. You said, 'Jan can NOT.' We kept on for a long time. Finally I pulled your hair, I couldn't help it. But you just said, 'Jan can't.' I did what I never did before and I pulled your hair several times. But you just said, 'Jan can't.' I got sweaty and hot. I was so bitterly sorry I started it. You just said, 'Jan can't.' You began to cry and we both cried so the tears ran. It must have been a wonderful sight, but we were completely alone in our struggle and no one saw us. In the end you picked up the cookie, but not until I slapped you several times. You stood up all of a sudden and put your arms around my neck and said, 'Jan is Grandma's nice little boy.' 'Yes, you certainly are,' I said and I cried too. Then you ate a proper meal and were nice and happy as usual. The next day when I went to the cupboard you came running and said, 'Nice Grandma, may Jan have a ginger snap?' and you got it. Then you said, all by yourself, 'Jan won't throw that cookie either.' I remember that well and I often laid awake at night and worried about whether I did the right thing that time, or if I was too hard. I did what I thought was right."

"Don't worry, Grandma. It was probably right."

I often wondered about how she saw me. We had conflicts later. She was very strong-willed.

"No, you don't," she said. "Here I'm the one who decides. And it's just as well you know it."

But I could never really do wrong in her eyes. Whatever happened and whatever I did and however much the others yelled at me, she was ready to think I did right. She would wonder and she would lay awake at night and worry, and she would sigh and she would even begin to cry so I had to tell her sharply to stop it. But whatever the others said she couldn't ever see any real fault in me.

Aunt Elsa showed me a letter the other day. Grandmother

had written it in 1940. I had just arrived home in Sweden from
New York and was sour at the whole world. They had left me
with my Uncle Robert, who then was Rector at Marieborg Folk
High School. All the cousins were there and Grandmother
supervised them.

"The children have so much fun. Mats and the girls are
mostly together. Fun for him to have company. And Jan is so
nice. He is the easiest of all to take care of. That's for sure. He
is also the oldest."

At that time Grandmother must have been the only one
who saw me that way.

In late fall 1946, Birgit left me and I was very sad. She was
the first girl whom I had really lived with, and not just slept
with. I went up to Grandmother at Säter. I read Sandemose and
wrote poems. Then she said to me one day at lunch:

"You think I'm an old lady, don't you?"

"No, not really."

"You think I'm senile and sentimental, don't you?"

"No," I said. "I don't think that."

"Yes, you do," she said. "Yes, you do."

Alva is blonde. Grandmother is dark. They had different
voices and different appearances. They were different types. I
have been married three times, but none of my wives have
been blonde, and none have been the same type as Alva. None
of them have had her cold flute-like voice, either. When I think
about it, I notice I have almost never been with a blonde. I
don't like blondes. Only two have been blondes. In spite of
everything there haven't been so many that I can't remember
them. My relationships with the two blondes didn't last.
Mistakes.

Now Gun is 56 and she is actually a lot like Grandmother
as she was when Grandfather died in 1934. She is the same age

as Grandmother at that time. There is a similar look around the eyes. The hair color and length and style are the same too. Both come from the North. Their stock is similar and family background, too. Gun doesn't cry easily. Grandmother did that only later when she was almost 70 and mostly with me. Otherwise she was known for her toughness and strength.

Even Mela who took care of me a lot in those years at Gesta was dark, like Grandmother. The imprinting of these early childhood years at Gesta determined that as an adult I would only go with and marry women with a certain look and a certain manner. Those with dark hair and voices that were not piercing. That I was so imprinted at Gesta is not strange. We all are imprinted as children. The child is the father of the man. But that does not mean that I sought Grandmother in love relationships and marriage. What I sought was, as far as I can understand, formed much later, from the age of twelve or so.

There are certain women I respond to as soon as I see them and I see them at a party, at a meeting, as soon as I come into the room. They stand out clearly from the others. A certain manner. A certain bearing. Move a little bit differently from the others. They have a special kind of timbre to their voices. I cannot say that they are like each other, but there is something about the mouth or a certain look or a frankness which they have in common. It is not makeup and it is not hairdo. Some are like that only a few short months as teenagers. Others become like that after bearing five children and I meet them 25 years later and they have not changed at all, even though the face is different.

I've never talked about this with anyone and I haven't gone around and bumped into them or tried to seek them out or anything. It is not even like falling in love. It is just that I know they are women with whom I could live. I see them. The others don't cause any emotional reaction, except those to whom I react negatively. It has been like that since I was a teenager and I assume it is like that for everyone. But I have not discussed it, and I didn't think anyone had noticed it until Gun said:

"Yes, that is one of your girls." We had lived together for ten years then.

"What do you mean?" I asked.

"I am pretty observant," said Gun. "I know you so I see them almost before you see them yourself."

I was embarrassed. I must have blushed. It was as if she had opened a peephole and looked inside me. We don't usually do such things. If you live together you should not analyze each other or display too much interest in each other that way. You should respect each other's integrity. There ought to be boundaries to intimacy, and trust, if a marriage is to survive. When you begin to speak too freely you have taken the first step toward a divorce. I know that from experience. It is not the first time I have been married.

"They don't know you. They don't notice," said Gun. "The only girls who will notice are the ones who make you uncomfortable. But that is not their fault. They haven't done anything. That is why I see to it that you are extra polite and courteous to them."

Since then we have not talked much about that. But what I react to are features I have decided on, or which were decided for me, in novels and drawings and paintings from the age of twelve on. Films mean less, even if Barbara Stanwyck maybe played a role for me. Twelve, I write. I read *Lorna Doone* then. Nelson Wheeler lent it to me. We went to the same school and he was a neighbor of mine in New York. He had grown up in China.

We are imprinted during childhood, but we choose at the

beginning of adulthood. There is a difference between the two. Gesta imprinted me, but I cannot reduce 1982 feelings to 1930 experiences.

That is probably right. But I awoke in the night and thought about Lorna Doone and wondered why I had chosen to name just that novel. Then I went down to the workroom and took out the volume. I had not read it in forty years. R.D. Blackmore wrote a marvelous novel more than 110 years ago. But I wonder about the twelve-year-old Jan Myrdal because when the hero, John Ridd, is fourteen years old he falls into the hands of the villainous Doones. He is saved from their claws by Lorna Doone, who is only a child. When he has grown, he searches for her. He hates the Doone family who killed his father. He protects Lorna from them and marries her in the end. Lorna Doone reminds me more of my childhood Stella than of the women to whom I respond today.

It is not Grandmother who imprinted the experience of Lorna Doone on the twelve-year-old. Who and what did that, if anyone at all, I don't know. Through that peephole I see nothing. It is only night and blizzard.

CHAPTER 14

One spring day a Zeppelin glitters high up in the air. It comes over the lake and continues on toward France. It was in Versoix. The air was high and clear and you could see Mont Blanc. The adults were around me in the yard. They pointed and I remember the word. Zeppelin.

This belongs to the earliest group of my recollections. It can be dated. All images from Versoix must have been from the fall of 1930 or spring of 1931. Those from Gesta can be as late as 1933 or even 1934 when I was almost seven years old. But the Zeppelin, that glittering spring day, glided out over Lac Leman when I was not quite four. I remember the yard and the house. It was white, two stories high and had a black balcony with wrought iron railings and green shutters. From the dining room you came directly out into the yard through tall glass doors. I had a pedal car too. A big car. I drove around on the garden paths. Mela sat in a lounge chair and read. Sometimes she put the book down on the lawn and sunned herself. She was there to take care of me, but also to rest. She had been sick. There was a nursemaid too. I don't remember her name. She walks with me on a path. We have come out from behind the walls and there are no houses. There is a field around us and the mountains in front are snow covered. It is spring and it is windy. The wind blows right in my face and I am angry and blow back and I say:

"Je suis fatigué."

She doesn't listen to me. She holds me by the hand and we continue to go toward Versonnex. I cry out:

"Je suis fatigué."

But she just continues to walk. I toot and toot like a boat in the night and dash back and forth after her like a dinghy on its rope while she holds my hand. I have gone boat riding often, even over the ocean. A cold wind is blowing.

I know that we drove around France, for there are pictures of me at the Pont du Gard and at the Pope's palace in Avignon and jumping on the benches at the arena in Nîmes, but I have not seen them in ages now. I do not have my own recollections of anything like that. The only thing I remember of the car is Gunnar driving very fast on a narrow winding gravel road high up in the mountains. He talks about how if the mail bus comes he must drive over on the outer lane. The mail bus always has the inner, whether it is the right or left. I sit in the back beside Mela. I am sitting on the outside. Alva and Mela call and say:

"Please, Gunnar. Drive a little more carefully."

But he only laughs and I toss around in the back seat and suddenly we skid into a ditch and I fall toward the door and the door flies open and I fall out. When I wake up again the car is stopped against a telephone pole down in the ditch. Above it are the Alps, all white. I am bleeding a little. I have hit my head and Gunnar says:

"Don't act silly."

Since then I have had a scar on my forehead. A triangle. As if I had been branded. The scar shows when I get cold and chilled or when I get angry.

I got new boots when I left Sweden. They were rubber. They were black and shiny. I sit on the wall at the lake. I have climbed up there myself. There are no adults in the yard. Then I take off my right boot and let it fall into the water below me. Our yard goes all the way down to the lake. I watch the boot bob on the waves. Then it fills with water. It drinks in the water gulp after gulp. Then it turns and tosses around and sinks away.

Afterward the grownups are very upset. They ask me all the
time what I did with the boot and I say it is gone. They look
everywhere. They ask me over and over. Finally Gunnar says:
    "The damn kid. He must have thrown the boot in the lake."
    But I don't answer any questions. I just say:
    "The boot came off."
    Here in Versoix I drink wine mixed with water with my
meals. That's what they do here. They also have sugar on their
sandwiches. First they spread butter on the soft bread. Butter
doesn't have any taste, so they put sugar on top.
    I don't remember my room in Versoix. Of the French I
spoke in the kitchen and with the nursemaid, I remember only
that I could say I was tired, but no one paid any attention to
that. There were no other children to play with, as far as I
know. The Zeppelin appeared again in drawings I made several years later. It sparkled and glittered high up in the blue, and
glided away over the lake toward France.

CHAPTER 15

Harry and I made a hiding place for treasure under the playhouse. The playhouse stood on a flat base, four stones which had been painted white. It was possible to crawl under it, even if it was tight. There, right under the floor, we had our hiding place. We had dug out a hole and filled it with flat stones. We plundered all the villages for miles around, and the sky shone red with burning houses when we returned heavy with plunder and we crept in under the playhouse to hide the booty.

We collected keys to all the houses of the manor and hid them. It took almost half a day because we had to sneak from room to room and hide ourselves well so no one saw us. We took key after key from the doors, and the cabinets, and even from desks and boxes. We emptied the whole house of keys. No one had seen us. We had stayed hidden behind clothes in the closet when Grandfather came by and we heard his steps. They were heavy. Then they continued away toward the stairs without him seeing us. There was a huge uproar in the evening when all the keys were gone. I was interrogated. I had to tell the truth, that all the keys were in the hiding place under the playhouse. None of the grownups could crawl in under the floor. In the end, they had to ask me. I crawled in under the playhouse while they all stood and watched. In there I got the keys out of our hiding place. But not all the keys were found. They said several of them were missing. I don't know what happened to those keys.

The next morning I was inside with Grandfather in the office. He was working on the accounts. He had a little silver cup on the desk to his right. He asked why I had taken the keys.

"We were just playing," I said.

"But why did you take and hide the keys?"

"It was booty that we captured," I said. But he didn't really understand what I meant. He looked at me a while and then he continued to write. He blotted with a roll of green blotting paper, but beside the roll of blotting paper there was a brand new blotting paper which had come in the mail. It was not particularly large, about the size of an oblong envelope. On one side you didn't blot and the paper was all white and smooth. There was a picture of a farmer walking through newly plowed fields. He had boots and a big vest and a moustache and looked strong and energetic. I looked at the picture. I leaned over the desk.

"Go out and play," said Grandfather. "I'm working."

He saw that I was looking at the picture. He took the blotting paper with the picture and gave it to me and said:

"Here it is. Now go out and play."

I went up to the upstairs hall. It was raining a little outside. It was drizzling. I did not want to go out. I took out the cows and horses and fences and gates and built a farm in the corner by the stairs. I placed the blotting paper with the picture against the bannister. He was a farmer there on the farm. Edith walked by. Grandmother walked by. She was busy with the linens. They had been washing. Then she came back up again and looked at me.

"Are you playing farm?" she said.

Suddenly she bent down and took the blotting paper. "That you are not supposed to have," she said. She became angry and went downstairs. She went to Grandfather's office. I leaned over the stairs, put my head between the posts, and watched her open the door and heard what she said.

"Don't you have an ounce of shame in your whole body?" she said. "You give this to the child? 'Drink aquavit made from Swedish agricultural products.'"

Grandfather answered, but I didn't hear what he said. Grandmother was angry, and she said:

"You are old enough to have some common sense. He can't read, you say, but others can read."

Then she closed the door and took the blotting paper to the ceramic tile stove. She ripped it apart and set fire to the pieces. She closed the door. First the black hatch and then the shiny brass cover. It was no fun to play with the farm any more. I picked up the figures and put them in their box. Then I went to the window and looked out into the drizzle.

It was true that Grandfather drank. No one had told me that and they never talked about it when I was listening. If they were talking about it they started to talk about something else when I came into the room. But he drank, and I knew it. He did not drink so that he fell down or slurred his words or acted like a drunk. Some did. But he had a silver mug beside him when he worked. When he came in after supervising the work, he went to the cupboard on the wall beside the door in the office. He opened the cupboard door, poured, and drank. He was often away at meetings and afterward there might be a party. Then he came home in the middle of the night or toward morning.

I was on the floor in his office looking at pictures in *The Farmer* one day when she came in. He was sitting at the desk writing. She said nothing. She went to the cupboard and opened it. It was as if she was counting the bottles. She took one of them out. It had lots of curls and flourishes on it. She held it up to the light. There was just enough in it to cover the

bottom. She sighed, put the bottle back and closed the cupboard door again. She looked right at Grandfather and sighed
again. I had never known anyone who could sigh that way. She
held her lips pressed together, looked at him, and sighed. He
sat completely still. She turned so her apron flew up and went
toward the door. Just as she began to close it he took the green
marble paperweight and threw it after her. It hit the door. But
she paid no attention to that. She turned as she closed the door
and sighed a third time. Then the door was closed and all was
quiet. After a while Grandfather noticed me. He breathed heavily.

"Your Grandmother is still just a sharecropper," he said.
"She will never get over it. She will never be anything more
than sharecropper trash."

He drank himself to death. He died because he drank. He
swelled up and they had to come and drain the water out of his
swollen stomach. But in his last years he only drank vermouth.
It was Dr. Renk in Strängnäs who told him that he would die if
he didn't stop drinking brandy and cognac. Then Grandfather
said:

"But a little vermouth once in a while for the stomach is
good for you."

"Yes, a little vermouth, maybe," Dr. Renk said.

After that Grandfather drank only vermouth. Uncle Stig of
Kvicksta, who was a boy then, said later that he was sent in
advance when Grandfather was planning to go to a party. Stig
had to bicycle ahead through the fields with the news.

"Pettersson from Gesta drinks only vermouth."

He had to repeat that to himself time after time when he
bicycled so as not to forget it. Vermouth was a word he had
never heard before.

As for me, I used to tell my classmates at Olof's School that

Grandfather died because he drank so much vermouth he was able to build a wall with the vermouth bottles as high as a man, from the big house to the hen house. But that can't have been true. There was no such wall. Actually, it was something I had heard when I was not supposed to be listening. Something I heard and believed literally.

Later, in 1937 or 1938, when I was ten or eleven years old. Grandmother used to talk about it. I sat on the bench in the kitchen while she washed dishes and we chatted.

"You are so sensible, Jan," she said. "I can talk to you about things."

"I lay awake at night and worry," she said. "I worry about whether I did right in not getting a divorce. But such things weren't done in those days and I believed that it was best to stay for the sake of the children. But it was so hard. We had a hard time with money and he was out at the bar and drank and then he came home and gave me a shameful sickness too. But I didn't want a divorce because of the children and now I don't know whether I did right or wrong. What do you think?

"Actually, he was not a bad man and he just wanted the best for us and in the beginning he never tasted a drop. When he came home with a bottle, he said, 'No, I won't touch it.' But when we went to Stockholm and he went into business, then he began to go along with the others out to the bar, and he had a right to it, and then it got worse and worse. Maybe I should have gotten a divorce. I had to stay home with the children and didn't get any money for the family while he was at the bar with friends and then they went to the girls.

"But he was actually nice and it was probably not easy for him. He never had any schooling or anything. Everything he knew he had to teach himself and that always stood in his way. The others had degrees and titles and everything. He probably wanted to show them that he was just as good, and he was too. He worked hard all the time. But he could not resist when they came to take him to the bars, and and that's the way it goes.

"Then in the autumn of 1914 he was in the militia and had a three-corner hat and kept a Browning down there in the drawer. They came one day and said, 'Now it's time, Pettersson. You've been called up.' He believed them and put on his three-corner hat, took his Browning, and went out. But it was only a joke. There was no mobilization and instead they all went to the bar. He was not really happy about that, even though he laughed along with them. He didn't like to be made a laughing stock or be fooled."

Grandmother had finished washing dishes. She sat at the kitchen table and drank coffee. She drank coffee through a sugar cube. She took a sugar cube in her mouth, poured the boiling hot coffee out of the cup onto the saucer and drank. People did that when there was no company. When she had drunk, she said:

"But he always wanted me to be elegant. He bought hats and silk dresses and when he was in the mood he came with presents for the whole family. But we never got to stay in one place. He built and sold and bought. Once we had a large flat at Valhallavägen, then a small apartment on the South Side. During the war we lived a while in a villa in Old Äppelviken and then out in the country. Every time he managed to get a farm and began to fix it up, we had to move on. It was not until we came to Gesta that he settled down. He fixed up Gesta too. He always wanted to work on it and make improvements.

"If he had had the chance to study, he would have had another kind of life, but it wasn't like that in those days. It wasn't his fault, really, that it went so badly with the booze. Others could tolerate it, but he got sick from alcohol and swelled up. It was something with the pancreas. Some inherited weakness.

"But everything was hard, and there was no one to talk to. I was so young when we got married, only a child. It was hard and poor at the beginning, and now I lay awake at night and worry about whether I did the right thing in not getting a divorce."

"Don't cry, Grandma," I said.

"But you didn't do that in those days and he was nice sometimes too, and had such a nice singing voice. We met in the lodge's choir and he had never tasted anything strong before he was 25."

CHAPTER 16

When there was a meeting, the men came and put their caps and hats on the black chest in the hall. Some came by car, others by horse and wagon. If it was winter and snowy, you couldn't hear the gravel crackle under the wheels as they drove up. Then the men stamped on the front steps before they came in. Edith helped them off with their coats or furs. Galoshes stood in a row under the chest. Some were new and shiny.

They came from the farms in the area, but sometimes someone came from Strängnäs and occasionally the pastor or the doctor or the teacher or the dairyman came too. Grandfather was having company. He greeted each and every one. He took them by the hand and welcomed them.

Then he sat all the men down at the oak dining table. They took out their papers and Edith came with a tray of mineral water and glasses. Grandfather sat at the short end of the table. He was the chairman. He banged the gavel on the table and the meeting had begun. All talk stopped. They spoke in turn with all the papers in front of them on the table. Afterward there was coffee. Then they drove away again. Sometimes a few stayed longer. They went into the library. Grandfather took out the cognac and Edith carried in water and glasses. Then they sat and smoked and talked at the brass table.

Grandfather was a Freemason and a Conservative and on the council and on the highway board and in the growing Farmers Union movement. He was well respected and they still remember him, even though he died in 1934. In the town book, *Toresund in Södermanland: History and Stories,* Eric Blomqvist wrote in 1970:

NOTABLES IN THE TOWN.

In all my years in Toresund, I have met many people.
Many have been forgotten and a few remain in my memory. Those who are called notables these days, one
remembers best, of course. One of these was C.A.
Pettersson of Gesta, nicknamed Gesta-Pelle. Gesta-Pelle
was a Farmers Union man who dared to have his own
opinions and could wield a gavel as few others. His political leaning was to the right, the old Conservatives, and
probably he was not loved by everyone. It may have been
the father's extreme leaning to the right that led his son
Gunnar to the Social Democratic party in the 1920s and
1930s.

Eric Blomqvist also wrote a few words about me:

During the first two or three years of his life, Jan stayed
with his Grandfather and Grandmother at Gesta. When he
got hold of his Grandfather's flint-lock pistol, he could
completely terrorize many of the ladies on the estate.

I don't remember the pistol, but it must have made an
impression on me because in 1958 in Kabul I bought a real
flint-lock pistol with inlaid mother-of-pearl for my son and
sent it to him in Sweden with a traveler I met in Herat.

I went along when Grandfather had errands down at the
carpentry shop, but I had to restrain myself so that I didn't get
into trouble or get in the way or interrupt a conversation. I had
to trot along beside him because he walked with a long stride,
but he held my hand and talked to me:

"Do you see how the road swells when the frost melts in
the ground"?

Occasionally I got to go along when he went to Strängnäs.
"No, the boy doesn't bother me. He's just keeping me company."

I sat beside him in the front seat. Most of the time he sat
quietly while he drove, but sometimes he sang:

Betänk dig, arme syndaträl:
Var vill du din förskräckta själ
För Herrens blickar gömma?

Think, poor thrall of sin:
Where would you hide your frightened soul
From the Lord's sight?

Then he became quiet and continued to hum while he
drove. Sometimes he also said something to me:

"Do you see the cathedral's tower? Thomas was bishop
there five hundred years ago. Thomas Simonsson. He was a
friend of Engelbrekt Engelbrektsson. In those days the kings of
the Kalmar Union between the three Nordic lands filled the
land with foreigners and set sheriffs over them to oppress the
people and kept Danish and German soldiers in Sweden. But
Engelbrekt aroused the people. He saw to it that we got a real
parliament representing all free men instead of mere lordly
Diets. We have him to thank for Sweden being a free land."

When we drove into the boulevard toward Strängnäs,
Grandfather sang for me Bishop Thomas' song on that
Engelbrekt rising of 1432 and our national war of liberation:

O ädla svensk, du statt nu fast
Och bättra thet som förra brast,
Tu lat tig ej omvända.
Tu vage tin hals och sva tina hand
Att frälsa titt egit fädernesland!.
Gud ma tik tröst väl sända.

Oh thou true Swede, thou standest now firm.
And mende that wherein thou didst fail
Thou shouldst not let thee be turned!
Stake thine neck and also thine hand
To save thine own true fatherland!
So God may cheere thee well.

There was sun on the streets and a blue sky.

When we were in the lobby of the bank I got to sit on an oak sofa with a black seat and black leather cushions at the back. The leather was cold. When he came out of the office Grandfather was in good humor. He took me to the pastry shop. He drank coffee with a Danish roll and I got strawberry juice and a pastry with lots of cream on it. When Grandfather looked at his watch, the little gold Freemason insignia dangled from the chain. But he did not want to explain what it meant.

"You will get to learn about that when you are big," he said. "I will see to it that you are accepted. I did that with Gunnar and that has been useful for him."

It was already late afternoon when we drove home to Gesta again. Now the leaves on the boulevard cast long shadows across the road. Grandfather said to Grandmother later, when we got home:

"Here's the boy. He has been nice and helpful."

Grandfather was a respected man. They greeted him everywhere. He decided that a new old people's home should be built beside Toresund church. And he was the one who drew up the plans. It was Grandfather who took responsibility for the Stallarholm bridge to Selaön. He had pushed for building the bridge. There was strong resistance to it, but he pounded the gavel on the table and decided. When the bridge was finished, Prince Wilhelm came with the governor to dedicate it. In the newspaper there was a picture of Grandfather and Prince

Wilhelm, who took each other by the hand on the new bridge. But there were other newspapers in the cupboard also. In one of them there was a crude black headline across the whole page. There was an oval picture too, a photograph of Grandfather. Landowner C.A. Pettersson, it said under the picture. But the big black headline which went across the whole page said: **Stallarholm's Mussolini.** It had to do with the bridgebuilding.

"These hack journalists write what they're paid to write and have the understanding to write. The bridge was needed. You can't put things off forever. Private interests must give way to the common good. When a bridge is needed, someone must take responsibility and see to it that the job is done. It can't be helped that some people will have their toes stepped on and begin to yell. The bridge is there."

The problem was that the legal expropriation had not been done when the building of the bridge began. It is said that one of the opponents to the bridge went away for a week to attend a funeral out on Gotland. He came home one evening when it was already dark and everything seemed to be as usual. When he woke up in the morning and raised his window shades, he saw a big new concrete bridge pier in front of him in the middle of his yard and the apple trees had been cut down.

Maybe that was why Grandfather never got the Vasa Order when Stallarholm bridge was dedicated, while other Conservatives with sharp claws received their Orders when they got their bridges built. They said that he didn't get an Order because his trading company went bankrupt in 1909, more than a decade before he came to Gesta. But he was not the only one who went into bankruptcy. Others could get their Orders in spite of having come up out of poverty and business difficulties. But Pettersson at Gesta could not get an Order. He had gone in with the farmers and been patriotic, and become a landowner and Freemason and Conservative. He was trusted in the community, but never received his Vasa Order. It is possible that this hurt him, but I am not absolutely sure. It is also possible that it strengthened something in him.

"A strong stream makes its own waves through the sea," he used to say.

One day he stood in the door and watched while Grandmother was trying to discipline me.

"I don't want to," I said.

"Your will grows in the forest," said Grandmother.

"No," I said. "I don't want to."

"There is a difference between what you *want* to do, and what you *will* do," said Grandmother.

"I still don't want to," I said.

"You are stubborn, but I am older," said Grandmother.

The question was whether or not I should wear my sweater when I went out. Grandmother thought the sweater was necessary. I thought it was not necessary. I don't remember who won. I did not scream and neither did Grandmother. We just spoke to each other. But I remember that Grandfather said:

"There is grit in the boy."

Later, in the sixties and seventies, I met people who had known and worked with Grandfather when they were young. He had helped some of them get ahead.

"He respected men who could work," they said.

He too was respected, but not loved and liked by all. There were some who saw him as hard.

He died as C.A. Pettersson. This was fifteen years after his children had changed their name. When Gunnar started college and was going to study law, he changed Pettersson to Myrdahl after the farm his grandfather had held, Myres. All of Gunnar's siblings followed his example. Gradually the H disappeared from the name. It was simpler to be called Myrdal without an H.

But Grandfather kept the name Pettersson. He had left the village and had no place of his own then. And it would be several years before he bought Gesta.

It was a peasant culture and we were called by the small holdings to which we belonged. Our patronymic showed our place in the family and then we had a personal name. There are real farm names in the family background. The great grandfather was originally of Perers, the grandfather of Myr. My mother's father Gunners. On father's father's mother's side Bu. On mother's father's mother's side Grönings. My father's mother was of Knuts. But the old names could no longer be used. There was a law about that. Father's mother's brothers could not be called Knuts, but must called themselves Knutsgård. No one could be called Myr or Myres any longer. Father's father kept the patronymic Pettersson after his father Perers Petter Ersson when the children changed to the more elegant name Myrdahl.

But Gunnar did not just change the name Pettersson. He also became close to—or a member of—the activist neo-conservative student league, Heimdal, and the nationalistic youth organization Nationella Ungdomsförbundet. Though never, as some, an academic fascist. And during the twenties he became more and more the Dalarnian, the peasant boy from Solvarbo of the Gustaf parish. But he had never lived there and had not grown up there. It was Grandfather who had left the village and worked his way up as he moved from one position to another and changed jobs and farms. There were times when he was a Stockholm building contractor and there were times when he was a farmer in Uppland. Then he returned to Stockholm as a wholesaler, finally to become a landlord in Södermanland.

"It is almost true that Gunnar was born in Solvarbo in Gustaf's," said Grandmother. "At that time we were still registered there. But your Grandfather was building railroads then and Gunnar was born in Skattungbyn in Orsa in a little cottage on the road coming from the station. We lived there with a family called Nissapers."

But the more the years passed the more Gunnar became the authentic Solvarbo boy from Myres Farm. Sometimes Grandmother said:

"I was born Anna Sofia Karlsson," she said. "Not Karlsdotter. It should not be written that way. My father was called Carl August Mattsson. But my mother was born Andersdotter after her father Orrbo Anders Ersson. But Karlsdotter was never my name. There were no daughter-names any longer when I was born, only son-names."

She saw to it that the information was correct in *Vem är det*. But she could not read English and in the *International Who's Who* it says:

"Myrdal, Karl Gunnar . . . born 6 December 1898, Gustafs, Dalecarlia: s. of Carl A. Pettersson and Sofie A. Carlsdotter."

When Grandfather died he was buried in Gustafs. There in the cemetery with a view of the valley they all rest under iron crosses and gravestones. Perers and Myres and Knuts and Orrbos and Gunners and Skräddars and Grönings and Knäpps and the whole large congregation who had lived honorably and died as Christians. Now Grandfather lay there too. His grave was the largest. It was a whole plot in the cemetery. On the heavy stone was written in gold letters:

Landowner Carl Adolf Pettersson's Family Grave
*Gustafs 4/4 1876
+Toresund 21/1/1934

In the summer of 1982 I went to the grave in the month of July. We had driven up from Fagersta. The air was heavy with thunderstorms far away. I had not been there in nearly two decades. I walked up the gravel path toward Grandfather's grave. He had chosen to rest there. There was a free view of the area.

But something had happened to the grave which I would never have believed could happen. Now there is an inscription in small and modest letters on the gravestone over his mouldering body:

Husband and Wife
1876-1934 Carl Adolf and Anna Sofia 1878-1965
Pettersson-Myrdal
Born in Solfvarbo

I read these words on the stone over and over again. Even Solvarbo has been given the old spelling. It looks almost authentic. My rage is such that I lose my breath. I can barely get air.

I remember Grandmother. We must have stood here at the grave in 1940. She was called Myrdal then. She changed her name from Pettersson to Myrdal when Grandfather was dead and buried so that people would not wonder how Mrs. Pettersson could be the mother of Professor Myrdal.

"'Building Contractor' would probably have looked better," she said.

That was what her brothers had said to her. On the stone he was described in gold letters as Landowner, and rested among the poor relatives.

"Landowner does look strange," she said.

But now she is dead too and above the two of them the heavy stone bears the inscription : "Husband and Wife Pettersson-Myrdal, born in Solfvarbo."

As I walk down toward the car I notice that I am soaked. The rain was pouring down on the graves.

CHAPTER 17

On April 11, 1927, three months before I was born, Gunnar defended his dissertation brilliantly. "The Problem of Price Determination and Variability." He was his professor's favorite student. He was a great scientific talent and the dissertation was groundbreaking. It also received the highest possible grade and Gunnar became a lecturer in national economy and finance at Stockholm University. His international reputation was growing and he was on his way to one of the great scientific careers of his generation. Grandfather had succeeded.

A miss is a good as a mile. Almost doesn't count. He who does not reign and win serves and loses. By much slothfulness the building decayeth; and through idleness of the hands the house droppeth through. Gunnar had been lazy and careless his first term in secondary school. It was then Grandfather talked to him and said:

"Either you become first and best and greatest, or you go out like a slave. In between there is nothing."

Gunnar became the best. He was, after all, gifted and Grandfather knew it.

They were not poor at home. But there was often a shortage of cash. Aside from whether business was good or bad, aside from whether C.A. Pettersson was at the top and made millions—at least on paper—or he went broke, nothing was allowed to disturb Gunnar's studies. Nothing was good enough for him who undertook to become first, best and greatest. There was no talk of the sisters continuing their studies. They were just girls and their duty was to admire their brother and take care of practicalities for him if he wished. Besides, father couldn't afford it. Gunnar had graduated from secondary school, started university studies, changed his name and was kept by Grandfather in a two-room apartment with a maid.

Gunnar was first-born and grew up during the family's most difficult years. Grandfather had not belonged to one of the more affluent families in Solvarbo. On the contrary. Grandmother, on the other hand, was a miller's daughter. Great-grandfather had owned a water mill. When Gunnar was born Grandfather was 22 years old and had just started to make his fortune. Grandmother had just turned twenty. She used to say that Gunnar was born two months early. I believed that Grandmother and Grandfather had to get married because she was expecting a baby. Couples used to get married when the girl got pregnant. While Gunnar was growing up Grandfather rose from village poverty to the middle class and entrepreneurial life and on up to the upper class and manor life.

It was Grandfather who wanted Gunnar to study law. Grandfather needed legal advice and tax shelters. Gunnar was good at that. It was also Grandfather who wanted Gunnar to be interim mayor in Mariefred. Gesta-Pelle liked the idea of a son as Mayor Myrdal in the city hall which baron Carl Cronstedt designed for Gustav III.

Grandfather, who had lifted himself out of poverty, was a Conservative. He was active in the farmers' movement. He was also one of the 32,000 men of the so-called national peasant levies from the 24 provinces who gathered in the courtyard of the Stockholm castle listening to the speech that Sven Hedin had written for Gustav V at the time of the attempted conservative coup d'état in 1914. He read the national poets, recited Heidenstam and Karlfeldt and had reproductions of Carl Larsson on the wall. Gunnar went over to Heimdal and was a nationalistic student. The brilliant neo-conservative theoretician and founder of geo-politics Rudolf Kjellén influenced his world view. He still does. Gunnar has never made a secret of that. Kjellén is more significant than Marx for Swedish Social Democracy under the Welfare State. As Gunnar continued his studies he acquired more distinguished and influential friends. He started to move away from the Right and into the freer academic Left. It was as a young radical, rebellious, with a curl on his forehead and a steady gaze, but at the same time an industrious, scientifically sound and respectful academic, he was loved by his teacher Gustav Cassel.

In the presence of his teachers and the new academic colleagues who were themselves in the process of making their careers, Gunnar never let on about his siblings and parents. He didn't even mention the younger brother who had begun to study classical archaeology. When Gunnar talked about his family he talked about Solvarbo and the Swedish peasantry and the relatives Grandfather left behind when he began to climb up out of the village about the time Gunnar was born. In Stockholm Gunnar turned himself into a boy from Solvarbo who had shown talent and got to study.

Following the dissertation and the brilliant defense there was a doctoral celebration for teachers and colleagues. Formal dress and speeches in Latin. But Gunnar invited neither his father nor his mother. It wouldn't be appropriate. Grandmother had silk dresses now and could both read and write and had a large circle of friends at the manors around Toresund, but she was not presentable. She would start to cry. She would start to talk. And with her it was as Grandfather said: the sharecropper trash shows through from behind the flowered hat. And Grandfather certainly had a tuxedo and was used to making speeches, but he was an upstart and a Pettersson. He would drink too much. He would get emotional. He would make an embarrassing speech.

"My dear boy," he'd begin, and then there was no telling

what else he would say in front of Gustav Cassel and Bertil Ohlin and everyone. He had to stay home. He wasn't invited.

But at Gesta Grandfather got dressed up in his tux and raised the flag and Grandmother had to put on her silk dress. At the liquor store in Strängnäs he had bought a bottle of the Yellow Widow, the sweetish Veuve Cliquot Goût Américain champagne, and he toasted with Grandmother and it was a great day because he had invested the family's capital in Gunnar. The speculation was a success and now Gunnar was on his way to world fame. Grandmother wept from emotion.

"I couldn't hold back the tears, he was so proud."

And they stood alone in their best dress in the living room and toasted their first-born who was having a party in Stockholm for teachers and members of the academic community.

Forty-seven years later, in 1974, Gunnar wins the Nobel Prize in economics. He should have won it the year before. He is worth a whole prize but has to share one. He has to share it with a rival he loathes. I sit at Fagervik and look at a photo of the ceremony in a newspaper. He is bent. He has started to have difficulty walking. The old hip injury is painful. He accepts the prize from the king and none of his children and none of his grandchildren wanted to come to the ceremony. He has no descendants. It was bitter for him. He got permission to invite a nephew, who had become director in the Employers' Association, and his siblings so he wouldn't be entirely naked and without family.

Gun bent over my shoulder and looked at the picture in the newspaper.

"Yes," she said. "So it went."

"That's the sort of thing Linnaeus called *Nemesis Divina*," I said.

CHAPTER 18

One late winter day I drowned. It happened as February turned into March. The winter had been warm. There was never any real chill. Now the days were getting longer. It was already starting to be light in the morning and when I looked out through the window there were banks of fog over the canal and street and they hid Karlberg Palace. The haze cleared slowly to let the ice appear.

In the winter a channel was broken in Karlberg Canal. Barges were towed through it. When we had moved back home to Sweden and came to Kungsholmstrand, I began jumping on the ice floes. It was a sport for the big boys. I followed them out onto the ice. The sun flashed on the ice. The snow was white. It made the eyes water. The air was clear and the sky blue. I was standing out by the channel. The big boys had already jumped across. Ice floes float in the channel and scrape each other. The boys leap from floe to floe. The object is to be first. But it doesn't count until you get back again. I look at them and there is a fresh wind over the city and we all laugh and shout. I am wearing my brown teddy bear jacket. Grandfather bought it. I jump out to get across the channel. I am the smallest. I am five.

It is important to keep on jumping. You can't stop and look around. You feel it in the feet and legs because the floes glide and dip into the water. If you stood still, the water would come up over the floe. That is why it is easy to jump when the channel is newly broken and the floes lie beside each other and scrape. It becomes more difficult as the floes get smaller and it is most difficult out at Riddarfjärden when the channel is so wide it is almost open water. There you can jump out toward the open water and then turn and throw yourself from floe to floe. They sink down all the time and glide away toward the open water until you reach the edge of the ice again. But the first time I jumped it was easy. Then the channel was narrow and newly broken and in the cold, water froze on my cheeks.

"Hi, Jan, hi!," the big boys called.

I don't think Alva and Gunnar ever knew I jumped. I told them once but they probably didn't understand what I said. In a way, it was not dangerous to talk to them about things like that. They didn't notice. Mary, on the other hand, was dangerous. She had seen me through the kitchen window. She yelled at me. She said I could drown and die. She told me about boys she knew who had drowned in the channel and never came up until much later when they were dredged up from the bottom with an anchor chain. They were black and swollen and smelled.

But I continued to jump in the winter. I got to be good at it. A few of us could feel how solid the floes were and could jump all the way out and still make it. Other boys who started thinking about it checked their jump, went down and had to be pulled up.

Now the ice was bad after a warm winter. I had not been out in it. It was gray and muddy and porous. The fog rolled in under the window, it was thawing and the air was raw. As I sat on my chair I was awakened by the chill. It was gray outside with a gray hazy light through the room behind me and everyone was sleeping. I walked through the empty apartment back to my room. Night was over. I crept down into the bed. The blanket was cold and damp.

On these mornings the air was clear. When I looked out everything was as sharp and clear as a picture post card. You could see the smallest details. The palace looked as if it had been clipped out of an issue of *Allers*. It was still early, not even six o'clock, but it was already light. Above the palace, the moon was red. It was almost perfectly round and red. The moon was always much bigger when it was down at the horizon. And now the channel was visible. It flowed through the ice. The floes were white. They danced.

I didn't jump alone. It was no fun and it was, in fact, dangerous. But now I go down the steps and the house rests quietly around me. Edvard Persson lives here in the building too. I have met him on the stairway. I had said hello to him. I had seen films in which he acts. Grandmother likes his films very much and I told him that and he asked me to greet Grandmother from him and I did. But I don't meet him now. He is sleeping too.

I am wearing my brown teddy bear jacket. But I am growing out of it now. When I open the street door no one is out there. Everything is still as sharp and detailed and clear as a photograph. It is not as mild and foggy as usual. It seems as though both eyes can now see the morning with equal sharpness.

When I walk toward the edge of the canal I see my tracks behind me, across the sidewalk and street. It must have snowed during the night. There is snow on the ground although it had been bare a long time. I hear my steps squeak in the snow. There are no other tracks. Not even a bus has gone by. I climb down to the ice. I wonder if it will hold. The weather this winter has not been good for jumping. The ice creaks. It cracks. It shakes under me and is muddy.

I walk towards the channel and the floes dance in front of me. The moon still hangs over Karlberg Palace, big and red and nothing is moving anywhere except the ice floes. I see no cars and no people and all the windows in all the houses are completely black. It is getting light now and the windows glitter and the houses turn red and the ice turns blue.

I walk further toward the channel and when I step onto the ice I stand still before taking the first leap. I hesitate, something one must never do, and the floe dips down into the water and I cannot get a good takeoff because water is already washing up over my boots. It is a poor weak hop and now I land heavily on the next floe and the water opens up. I fall between the floes and the ice glitters high above me and it is heavy and black. It is difficult with the teddy bear jacket and I wave my arms wildly to get up and it is cold.

I pull myself up. I have no ice stick and my hands glide over the ice and do not get a grip. Now I do get a grip because the ice is dirty and I can slide myself over the edge of the ice and walk home. I can get a hold so I can pull myself up. I lie on my back too, against the ice and kick the floe and push myself up and there are many ways to climb out. I have gone down many times. One night in the spring of 1946 when I was crossing Lejondal Lake at Bro to meet some girls I went down, but then I had a knife with me. I have gone down in cracks too, during the war when we jumped at Ålsten. Sometimes when you have gone down you do not know how you came up. You just did a sudden takeoff in the water as you felt the ice breaking and you push up out of the water without understanding how it could be done. First you walk on the ice. Then the crack opens and you go down. Then you push up. Then you stand on the ice again wet up to your hair and the dampness slowly begins to soak through your clothes and you freeze and run toward the shore.

But it's also possible that I didn't get back up. Maybe I couldn't. The stream pulled me under the ice and then I was gone.

Everything is very clear until the point when I try to get up out of the water. Maybe all too clear. The details are so sharp they are unreal. In fact, I jumped and jumped that winter day in

1934 although there were not many who did that. I went down with the teddy bear coat and it was the last time I wore it.

But that same spring I began to wonder whether I had drowned. Maybe the whole thing was so so sharp and clear because it was the last thing I remembered. They say that is how it happens. I also read how, at the moment of death, the eye photographs the reality around it and you are supposed to be able to catch a murderer by cutting out the victim's eyes and putting them under a microscope and lighting them with ultra-violet light. I do not know where I read that. Probably not in *Allers*.

If it was true that I went down and drowned then the last moment was stretched out. Time got stuck. It might be said that could not be true because so much happened afterward and I was still living. But how do I describe it? First it is the present and then suddenly it is another present. It is as if I blinked and I cannot actually prove that what I call memory and what I went through really happened. Back and forth I thought about how I might have drowned and was already at the moment of death when time stretched out and what I thought was the present was only an ice floe suddenly popping up as I disappeared.

I thought a lot about this. I couldn't find a way to prove that I really still existed. It often happens that you dream and you say you are dreaming but you say it in a dream you are dream-ing. It doesn't help to pinch yourself. You can dream that you pinch yourself and dream that you wake up but everything is just a dream. It might be the same with death. You die in a sin-gle moment down there in the water under the ice, but that last moment is stretched out and sticks and time congeals.

There was no one to talk to about this. I do not think I even tried. I knew it was pointless. They could not even understand that the earth was round. How could they seriously think about knowing you do not exist any more? Alva would come with tests and sit behind me and chirp and make notes. I did not want understanding and did not want to be comforted. With deep shame I remembered what had happened when I tried to talk with her about the people on the mountain. They sit on the Alps, one person on each peak, and while I told her about it her eyes were gray and cold. She began to chirp with her voice to comfort me and make me happy—as if that is what I wanted—and then she went into the study and made notes. No, she didn't want to think about how difficult it was to know if you were still alive and if you really existed. There was no one to talk to about such things. There probably never is for anyone, I thought.

Maybe it was that spring I seriously discovered that there was a great and secure freedom in this knowledge.

Suppose it was true that what I had experienced as the present was an ice floe quickly floating away in the long moment when time stood still and I died long ago in the water in front of Kungsholmsstrand. There was no reason to care whether Gunnar had bloodshot eyes and shrieked louder and louder while Alva stood beside him and chirped.

"He is a sadist," I said.

"No," said Alva, "you should not say that."

And they were not really there. I could close my ears and look them away until they were very small figures who gestured and hopped on the floor. They could not get to me.

Nearly fifty years later I still think about how I really should be able to prove to myself that I did not drown that time. The question can also be reversed. Maybe I have been dead for fifty years. However the question is put, it brings a great and secure freedom. It opens a back door to existence.

CHAPTER 19

In 1933, when I was six years old, I first traveled to Africa. But I made my big trip in the winter of 1934-'35. The drawings and stories from 1933 are difficult to read. The letters are reversed, as in a mirror, and upside down, and are scattered over the page without apparent connections. Or so it seems to others. I myself can still read them. Behind the almost impossibly indecipherable marks I see the pictures which are supposed to be visible. But in the winter when I was seven going on eight, I made trips which others could see too.

I wrote several books about this trip. Some I wrote in school. They have been colored. But they are dull and the color has been dutifully pencilled in. It is clear that the teacher tried to direct this free development of personality. They are subdued and irritable. "The Book of Jan," one is called. Another is called "A Trip to Africa."

But I wrote other books at home in the afternoon, sitting in my room. I had an old typewriter. Nobody thought they ever would be able to read my handwriting. I went to the movies a lot. The newsreels were good. There was a lot of war and catastrophe. But Tarzan was good too. There were also good movies from America with riding and shooting. In the books I wrote, I was with my classmates from Olof's School taking part in the things that happened in those movies. With corrected spelling, one of the books reads as follows:

FOREWORD

This book is an adventure story in the African jungles as experienced by Jan and Gabriel.

I

Once upon a time there were two boys who fought until they made up and then they decided to build a boat and they made the boat.

Then they made a flying machine and flew to the African jungle and there they landed and Jan shot a tiger and Gabriel threw a lasso around a zebra.

Then they built a hut and the next day a volcano erupted. When the volcano was over we met Ragnar and he said we should prepare for war with the savages.

When they came we shot down all the savages and then Göran came and said we should get ready to battle other savages and we answered that we had shot all the gunpowder and lost all the bullets. And when the savages came we beat many of them to death so the others fled into a house.

II

Two days later the volcano erupted again and then the savages came and 432 were left and we beat them to death and then on January 19, 1935, we went to our airplane and to the Indian jungle where we landed and built a hut and then we made cannons and then we made 2794 more cannons because they are broken and we did not want to be afraid they would break again.

Then a tiger killed Göran. Ragnar killed the tiger and then we ate the tiger meat for a week and then we went to the African jungle and then we caught baby tigers and we tamed them and they were our faithful servants.

III

Jan had a tank and Jan drove over Ragnar's airplane and Ragnar bought a tank and drove over Jan's airplane and Gabriel's airplane. Gabriel bought a tank and he drove over Ragnar's tank and Ragnar had to pay 2348 Crowns to Jan and Gabriel.

IV

The savages came the next day and we battled them and the next day was Sunday and Ragnar was killed by a python snake which became food for the lion and baby tigers and then came two cobras, which we killed.

The next day was Jan's birthday. The next day was Gabriel's birthday.

Then we went to Africa's capital city and from there to Sweden and from there to China and from there to India and from there to Abyssinia and from there to Germany and from there to Russia.

V

And then

The book stopped there. It was illustrated but not in color. Volcano eruption. Attacking airplane. The landing of paratroopers. Nests of machine guns with palms around them. The shots were represented by dots. Cities which were bombed. Big black-streaked explosions which blew enemies into the air.

It was a trip full of war. There were other versions of the trip to Africa too. They all began with the boat I built. Some of them were about desert islands and treasure. With great difficulty I drew death skulls and leg bones laid crosswise all the way up on every page in the book about pirates and Ragnar walking the plank. Some were about the jungle itself with vines and tall trees and lions and snakes so big they could swallow a lion whole and when you cut up the snake the lion was alive and became a grateful and nice lion who followed faithfully as a dog and threw himself on all our enemies and had large gold teeth that cut quick as lightning.

In shop class I built the boat I had written about. I spent all fall and winter building it. It got to be big. I could carry it with great effort. It needed to be properly equipped for the voyage to Africa. I collected newspaper clippings and pasted them in a scrapbook. The clippings were about the equipment needed for a trip to Africa. Under a newspaper picture it says, "I will put a chart room on an old scrap battleship."

The picture shows a wheelhouse used as an office in a London gas station.

There are also world maps and I must have thought about various projects because both the Atlantic and Pacific oceans appear in several versions. I didn't have a real globe. I wished for one and thought about having a big one. It would stand on the floor and I would walk around it and rotate it and look at where the countries and oceans were located. But I never got one. Instead I bought a pencil sharpener which was also a small globe. But the globe was very small.

The boat was finished in the spring of 1935. Then I painted it yellow. I was taking it to Kungsholmsstrand to launch it. I got the boat from school and pulled it to the streetcar stop. But I did not get to take the streetcar when it came. The conductor only laughed and held up his hand to stop me.

"You can't take that with you."

Then I started to carry the boat. I carried it all the way down Valhallavägen and then Odengatan and then St. Eriksgatan, over the bridge and down the steps to Kungsholmsstrand. By then it was evening and it was getting dark because the boat was heavy and I couldn't carry it very far without stopping to rest.

It was already spring. The ice had broken up long before. The leaves were green and the air was mild. A train went past on the other side. I got the boat off the sidewalk and into the water. It floated because it was made of wood. Then I jumped down into it. I was all alone on the water. The street lights had already been lit.

My feet went straight through the bottom of the boat. I sank with the boat. The water was cold. It was difficult to get away, but I took hold of a sewer pipe and got up on the sidewalk again. Now I was soaking wet and smelled bad from the sewer water in my clothes. Only scraps and splinters remained of my boat. I turned and walked home.

I don't know how I explained why I had been gone all afternoon and don't know how I explained why I was soaking wet, but I said nothing about the boat. I never said anything about the boat and the trip and I completely stopped writing stories about Africa. When the bottom went out, it was all over. I turned my back on it forever.

CHAPTER 20

I heard it on the number four streetcar. I was on my way home and stood on the rear platform of the front car. They must have gotten on at Odenplan. Maybe they came from the college. But I did not see them because I stood with my back toward them, looking out. I was not listening at first. It was mid-afternoon and the car was almost empty. There were only those ladies who got on at Odenplan and now cackled behind me. I began paying attention when one of them said:

"Yes, it's too bad about the Myrdals."

I did not dare turn around. I stood with my face to the window and heard them talk about me behind my back.

"He's such a problem child."

"Yes, she's very worried about him. He is difficult."

My neck went cold. I could feel the hairs on my neck stand straight out and it tingled. They were talking about me again. I got off at Dalagatan. I got out of the car sideways so they would not see me. When I was down on the street I looked up at them quickly. They were about 25 years old. Maybe thirty. I had never seen them before. They did not know me. They did not recognize me. The streetcar clattered on with them and I walked slowly through the park. When I reached Toy Grotto just before the bridge I stood a long time at the window and looked at all the toys. I had nothing left of my allowance and what I wanted to have was impossibly expensive. It was a steam engine. It was so big that it took almost half the space in the window. The boiler was shiny copper. The base was polished like a stone floor. The flywheel was painted red and black. I sometimes dreamed about that steam engine at night and could actually hear how it hissed and sputtered and see how the flames flickered behind the window.

They all talked about me. While I stood on the bridge and looked out over the canal I could think again about the ladies on the Number 4 whom I did not know but who talked about me. I was a problem child. They all said it. And I knew who had said it to them and who always said it. Grandmother did not say it. And not Mela. And not Elsa. But Alva and Gunnar said it. They said it to me. They said it to Mary. They said it to each other and to everyone they knew. I was not eager to go home. They were there. It was almost never pleasant to go home except in the mornings when they were not home. But then I was in school, of course, unless I could persuade Mary I was sick and got to stay home and play.

Now fifty years later, when I have children and grandchildren myself who all have different dispositions and personalities and peculiarities and are sometimes sullen and nasty and sour but still in most ways not so different from me in manner and behavior, I wonder whether it was really necessary to talk about me. In any case, I loathed it.

I sometimes stood up right in the middle of the room and just shouted, "Leave me alone! Leave me in peace!," when Alva talked about me with her women friends. She sat in the black chair and a friend sat in the yellow chair and Alva's voice sounded like a flute as she talked about my problems. I had come in and stood at the door listening. Her gray eyes rested on me a short moment. Now she talked about my sleeping problems. I pissed on myself in the night when I stood on the chairs at the window and looked out over the canal.

I screamed at her and at the other ladies to leave me alone.

"Yes, you can see for yourself. That is how he is," she said. And she sighed.

Against that I was completely defenseless.

I have never seen a child get such a bad reputation or get blamed, without any reflection on the adults. Now, a long time later, I believe that such talk was part of the open manner of the 1930s generation. They had liberated themselves from Grandmother's sentimentality. They opened themselves to each other by talking about their children like small nasty cases. Grandmother demanded evening prayers and table grace and washing hands and sitting quietly while the grownups talked, but she didn't talk behind my back. I still don't understand how Alva succeeded in talking about me that way without having the least shadow fall on herself.

It didn't happen to me only when I was five and six years old and unable to defend myself. It followed me through life. In 1956, when it began to be clear that Gun and I were more than friends, we used to go visit P.O. and Anne-Marie Ultvedt—who lived at Odenplan at the time—and drank coffee and talked about art. The autumn was chilly and my one-room apartment on Skånegatan was cold.

But Anne-Marie's older sister was worried about Gun when she heard Gun was going with me. I was awful. Such a pity for the Myrdals, to have such a son. She knew that because she had practiced at the Rolf Bergman household before the war when he was chief physician at the hospital. She needed practice before entering household school. Rolf Bergman was a classmate of Gunnar Myrdal, and Alva and Gunnar Myrdal were frequent visitors at home and they were so unhappy because of Jan. He was so difficult.

That is how it was. I could not defend myself against that when I was five years old and I do not understand it now that I am 55. In the meantime I have observed many families and come to know many children and—as I said—now have my own children and grandchildren. Such awful children as I was said to be do not exist. I have never heard people talk about how awful their children are without some of that awfulness rubbing off on themselves, but Alva and Gunnar succeeded. Maybe that was how people talked in their circle. Functionalism with plain talk and steel pipe furniture and white walls and talk about the nasty child who is kept in the messy nursery.

Or it may also have been just Alva's and Gunnar's personal characteristic. But after Grandfather died and Gesta was sold I was left helpless and could not defend myself from them.

The spring day in 1935 when the two unknown 25-year-old ladies stood on the back platform of the front car on the way from Odenplan to St. Eriksplan and talked about what a pity it was for the Myrdals that Jan was so awful and such a problem child, I was seven going on eight. I looked out the glass window and out there on the street messenger boys rode by on bicycles and cars drove past and people walked on the sidewalk and the ladies' voices twittered behind my back. It was not the first time I had heard such things from strangers who did not know who I was and who did not even consider that the seven-year-old in shorts and knee socks and polo cap who stood with his back to them and looked out at the traffic was just the case they were talking about when they felt sorry for for the poor Myrdals because of the boy.

At any rate I was a problem child. They all said so. That was why I went to Olof's School and that was why I now had to change schools. It was also necessary to separate Gabriel and me. We had a bad influence on each other.

It was Gabriel who got me to like Homer. We read him in the Children's Library edition. Gabriel always wanted to be Hector. I leaned mostly toward Achilles. Odysseus was good too. But I didn't want to be Agamemnon.

We also went to the railway museum. There were a lot of wonderful models there. We could look at them for hours. They were so well made. They were like the real thing, only small. Every little thing was there. There were locomotives from different times and there were cars with complete interiors and there was the South Side entrance to Stockholm and it was so fantastic to look at that it almost made the chest hurt.

We discussed at length how we could get hold of such a model. But we couldn't find a way. It was pointless to talk to the grownups, they wouldn't understand. Gabriel's grandfather was Hjalmar Branting. Maybe we could make use of that fact? Alva and Gunnar were also well known, but they were not dead yet. But we could't figure out how even Hjalmar Branting could help us get such a model. We just went back to the exhibits and looked again.

We discussed the Africa trip together. It was for the most part a shared fantasy. The whole school took the train up to Dalarnia on a ski trip and the last day of the vacation there was to be a masquerade. Gabriel was a pirate. He was dark, so it suited him. I was a pirate too, even though I was blond and the teacher wanted me to dress up as something else.

We stole toffees in a shop on Valhallavägen. But we never got caught so the grownups never knew. We were interested in some girls in our class. One was called Anne and she had long hair. She lived at Djurgårdsbrunn. We made up plans about how we would drop a coin in the washroom and then ask her for help picking it up. When she leaned over to reach out her hand and pick up the coin, we would lift her skirt and pull down her underpants. We never carried out the plans. But we pretended to lose a rubber eraser which we had to find right away and crawled around on the floor under the table to look under the girls' skirts. I had a little toy camera that could really take pic-

tures. But it was very small. It took special small film. We saved
our allowances and bought a roll and crept around on the floor
and photographed under the girls' skirts. Then we took the film
in for processing. We were very eager to see the result. But
there were no pictures. The negative was almost transparent.
There was almost no light under the table. But I don't think the
grownups found out about that either.

I don't remember that we were any worse than that. I wondered over the years whether there are large gaps in the memory, significant events that I had repressed. But I don't think so.
When Alva said that Gabriel and I had a bad influence on each
other I think she was really most irritated that we played and
had fun and that she had no understanding of what was so
much fun. Since leaving Gesta I had never had so much fun as
I did with Gabriel. We were heroes of the Trojan War and we
talked about pirates and we went and looked at the model
trains and we crawled around and looked for what girls had
under their skirts and there were a million things to do and talk
about. Alva didn't think of that. She thought it was almost as
strange as when I sat and talked to the old harrier Träff when
we were with Folke at Kvicksta.

I knew they were going to move me from Olof's School.
They had told me it was because Gabriel and I went around
together too much and had a bad influence on each other. I had
come home and almost forgotten what the two ladies on the
Number 4 platform had said. I sat on the floor in my room and
built. I was pretending the whole time. I sat and mumbled to
myself as I usually did when I pretended. I built a country with
cities and railways and factories and the country was at war
with another country and the kings fought and fell and new
troops marched around the walls. Then I heard the door open
behind me. My back got stiff and it hurt between my shoul-

derblades and I had trouble breathing but I tried to pretend I had not heard anything. It was Alva.

"Are you sitting here playing all alone, little Jan?" she said.

I turned around and drew my mouth into a smile and saw her gray eyes rest on me and now the whole game fell apart and it was as if a gray film had come over the room and everything was gone and there were just wooden models left.

Then she took a step back and closed the door again, but it was all over. I got up and kicked the wooden models away and went to the window and looked out at the yard. Twilight had already begun to fall.

CHAPTER 21

Sissela was born in December 1934. Grandfather had died eleven months earlier. I was just seven and a half years old. Gunnar told me I was jealous of Sissela. I felt as if I had been demoted from first place in the family, he said. It was a complex. He didn't just tell me. He told Mary. He told all the relatives who came to visit to see the little one when she came home. When Alva and Gunnar had dinner parties with their friends in the evening, I could hear how he told the guests.

I don't know whether it was true that I was jealous of Sissela. It was probably much more complicated than that. In their family I didn't have first place, I never had it and I didn't want to have it. But I never doubted for a moment that Sissela was their child. I never doubted it later either. But I thought it was less believable that I was theirs. I didn't belong in their home.

I felt at home at Gesta, but Gesta was sold. I felt related to Grandfather and Grandmother in some way. But Gunnar and Alva were strangers to me. They didn't think as I did. They didn't behave the same way. They didn't see the same things. And they didn't like animals. Sissela suited them. She was like Alva and, charmed, Gunnar would later give her the nickname "Little Hypocrite." It made sense that her first book, when she was an American and over forty, was about lies. She dedicated it to her husband, Derek. If I had written a book about lies and dedicated it to Gun, she would have filed for divorce. But we were different. Sissela is in every way a child of Alva and Gunnar. She is as phony as a three-Crown coin and always has been. She lacks her own style. But she probably sees it differently.

I think that Sissela, with her American blonde hair, rigid face and high voice from which small cold laughter comes unmotivated in the middle of a sentence, framed by her big house, is an improbably stereotypical Harvard president's wife. Others are charmed. The kind who were charmed by Alva in her time. And that is probably at the center of it. Sissela and Alva are very alike and I am a stranger to both of them.

I think it is correct to say, as Gunnar says, that I didn't like Sissela when she was born. But not in the way Gunnar described it to his friends. If I had been able to formulate it at the time I would probably have said:

"First Grandfather died. Then Gesta was sold and my childhood home was put up for auction. Then I went to Alva and Gunnar and was supposed to live with them. Then they got their own child."

Sissela had another name too, Sissela Anne. Why she got the name Anne, I don't know. But in December 1934 Alva said to me:

"We call her Anne too. Isn't that nice. You're so taken with that girl in your class."

I was cold inside from shame. I backed into the door, smiled and said:

"Yes, that is nice."

Alva could never notice anything without beginning to pick at it. However smooth and clean you were, she always found a little spot to pick.

I never had any parties at home. I never had a Christmas party. But I went to parties and Alva tried to get me to agree to having one at home. Gunnar said nothing about it. He didn't bother about things like that. But I never agreed to have a party. I would rather have people say I was stingy and inhospitable. I saw how Alva would act with the children and heard how she would chirp and I was ashamed in advance. There would be no end to the stories Gunnar could tell his dinner companions about little Jan and his friends. I would stand at the door in the hall and hold it a little bit open to listen and hear them eat and drink and Gunnar would tell funny stories about me and they would all giggle. It was like that already. How would it be if he saw me with my friends?

Late in the spring of 1935 we moved away from the city. Gunnar rented a house at Bromma. There was better air out there and we needed more space. Sissela was to have a nurse. There was no room for that in the apartment on Kungsholmsstrand. There was no special baby room either.

The house we rented was on Thaliavägen. It was number 41. The nearest train stop was Olovslund. The number 12 street car line went there from Tegelbacken. Bromma was far out. Only Nockeby was farther out, where there was new construction and Markelius put up his functionalist house. Gunnar had rented the house on Thaliavägen from an officer who was posted to Abyssinia, I think. In any case, the family had all their good furniture stored in the garage. We had no car. You didn't need a car in Sweden, Gunnar used to say.

I had often been in Bromma when I lived at Kungsholmsstrand. Construction of the Traneberg Bridge took many years, beginning at the beginning of the thirties. The barges which went past out on the canal carried gravel and stones to the construction site. We used to play out there. It was forbidden. But no one paid any attention to us as long as we were not in the way. We also went across the pontoon bridge to play on the Bromma side. There we climbed trees and one spring day just before we moved I sat lookout way up in a pine tree.

One time Elsa took me on a Sunday walk to see the villa
Grandfather built during the World War out in the suburb of
Äppelviken. It was a large villa with three floors. It was situated
among pines and from it you could look out over rooftops and
streets and water. But it was sold before I was born and we
were not going to live there. We moved much further out.

The villa on Thaliavägen was a large rough-sided wood
house. It was on a slope. The basement was a whole story high
on the road. When you stood and looked up at the villa it was
a three story house. Or rather—because the attic was so high—
a four story house. The second floor had an overhang. The
house was large, but it was not large in the same way Gesta was
large.

I can't say that I liked moving to Olovslund or that I disliked
it. The friends I had played with when the Traneberg Bridge
was being built and who were there playing on the other side
of the canal at Karlberg were just the kind of playmates you forget the day after you go away. I would never again see my playmates from Olof's School, Gabriel and Ragnar and the others.
We had a bad influence on each other. It made little difference
whether I moved to Bromma or got to stay on at Kungsholmen.

I can see the villa very clearly and in detail. When you came
into Thaliavägen from the Olovslund stop and walked up the
hill toward Höglandstorget, the villa rose on the right hand side
beyond the pines and park, or maybe it was just undeveloped
land. I can open the iron gate. I can walk the five steps up to
the first landing, and then the four steps to the vacant lot itself,
and from there walk up the remaining steps to the door. There
were eight steps and I stand in front of the heavy oak door with
iron mountings.

It has been twenty-eight years since I last went by there. It
was early in the spring of 1954. A Sunday when the snow was

melting. I stopped under the villa and pointed up at the window in the gable and said:

"That was my room."

Maj was walking beside me. She was my second wife. We had just returned to Sweden from Eastern Europe. She was dressed in the kind of Romanian peasant coat that became fashionable fifteen years later. We were taking a Sunday walk with Svend-Aage and Marta and their daughter Lena. Svend-Aage and I were discussing Bernard Shaw, I remember. Bernard Shaw and the labor unrest in Poland. He talked about the working class rising up against the bureaucracy and the new class.

"I lived here," I said.

I had stood behind those window panes as a child.

I can see us walking down Thaliavägen in 1954. I can see the villa in different seasons during 1935 and 1936. I can walk around it. I can see the glass doors, the big French windows facing the garden. I can stand in my room behind the panes in the gable window. But when I stand in front of the heavy oak door with the black mountings and open it, I see nothing inside. It is dark. It is like an old attic. It is like a deserted storehouse. A large dark space. With effort I see the stairway under my feet, and walk up the steps in the darkness with a weak flashlight. I see the door to my room. The white paint is peeling off the door. The door must have been blue before. I press down on the copper latch and now the room is well lit. I can see every detail. There is the bookshelf and there is the table and there is the bed and there is the box with all my things. The curtains are white and now the window is open and it is spring and I can see how they move in the draft. But behind me everything is empty and dark.

I have never thought about this before. I had assumed I could see the whole villa if I wished. When I passed by here in

1954 I saw the façade and pointed to the window and said: "I lived back there."

If I walk through the park, or the vacant lot, to Thespisvägen where Olle and Lennart lived I can see their villa. Olle and Lennart were brothers and my closest friends when I lived in Olovslund. I can walk onto their property. I can walk around the house. I can see the sandbox and the green rain barrel and their mother's kitchen garden and the garage where their father parked the car he bought in 1936 and then I can walk through their door and open it and enter and I can see their hall and there is the door to the basement stairs and then I walk into their kitchen and on into the dining room and I see the table and chairs and chandelier exactly as they were and the cupboard there on the wall. I can see the family room too with furniture and everything, only we were seldom in there, and I can go upstairs to the upper hall and there is a portrait of Chancellor Adolf Hitler on the wall for he was, they said there, in spite of everything, an important man—but that is a later story—and I know where their parents' bedroom is and can see it although I was in there only a few times and I can go into their room and I see it just as clearly as I see my own room on Thaliavägen.

But if I stand on Thaliavägen again and get ready to go inside, the black empty space echoes beyond the oak door. I walk around the house and stand in front of the glass doors. They shimmer now and the inside glitters and shines and to see what is inside I open the tall French windows, but inside is the same emptiness I found at the oak door. When I close the glass doors they glitter again and to look through them is like looking inside a room with bright light and mirrors.

I wonder about this. I go up the steps to my boyhood room and see the wood floor under my feet step by step. Then I stand in my room and look out through the window. I used to stand like this when I daydreamed. Or I lay on the bed and looked up at the ceiling. I liked to play catch then. With a bright candle or a bowling pin. Throw it up and catch it and throw it up and catch it while I daydreamed.

At that time, from 1935 onward, I never told anyone what I dreamed. I had stopped doing that back when we lived on Kungsholmsstrand. I taught myself to sit at the table and daydream or to sit at my school desk and daydream. It was just a matter keeping the eyes still. It was like hiding the eyes and keeping the mouth shut. Once in a while I tested carefully whether my lips were properly sealed. They stuck to each other. They had to do that to prevent a single word from slipping out.

Much later I would do the same thing when I sat with a girl whom I liked. But then it was different. Then it was a matter of not letting my face show what I was feeling while at the same time fleeting eye contact became a deep sigh throughout my body.

I stepped into a daydream when I opened the heavy oak door and walked into the large space. You could barely see that something was hanging down from the ceiling high above. But the daydream began in my room at Thaliavägen 41 in 1935 when I had just turned eight. It was not a frightening or dangerous fantasy and because of that I felt no anxiety now as I opened the oak door and saw nothing but darkness and emptiness. I just wondered.

There were different versions of that fantasy and they could be different lengths and play themselves out in different ways. It could be very long and detailed and full of surprises, but it ordinarily began in one of two ways.

Once upon a time there was a boy—me, of course—who

woke up very early one morning. It was so early that it was not even morning yet.

I got up and it was completely quiet in the whole house and it was quiet outside and if I looked out the window there was only a thin stream of light way out at the horizon.

When I opened the door and went out into the hall I realized I had awakened at the wrong time. That night I saw everything was actually very small. The doors stood open as if for airing and the other people in the house were in their beds. But when I looked more closely there were no people. They were dolls. A kind of automatic mannequin, turned off now for the night when they thought I was sleeping. I had awakened at the wrong time and walked into the hour I was not supposed to know about. But now I could see that the whole house and all the people and all the houses around were only a toy world.

It was terribly exciting.

I went out of the house and down to the stop and the streetcars were really toy streetcars. Everything was very well made. The intention was that I should not notice. During the day when they thought I was awake someone set the whole thing in motion around me.

Now I had come upon the secret and knew that it was only a toy world and I could do what I liked with it. Sure, the people I met during the day were finely constructed dolls who like dolls could say "Mama" when you turned them over. Just as there were ordinary toy animals which bellowed and brayed when you pinched them, these toy people made various intricate gestures and produced various sounds. When I sat in the streetcar on the way to school these dolls talked with each other. I listened to them. Sometimes the mechanism got stuck. Then the ventilators blew and air whistled in the pipes. Then everything returned to normal and the game continued.

I wrote that "someone" got the whole thing in motion around me during the day. It would be more correct to write: it was set in motion. I was not meant to discover how things really were. I didn't fantasize about who or what controlled this toy world. I didn't bring God into it. Not gods or powers in general either. Later, around 1938, I continued this fantasy. I sometimes made it into an even more exciting story about how a boy wakes up one night at the wrong time and discovers that he has awakened when the play is over. He is able to walk around in it and little by little discover everything until he finally comes out of the play and onto the tabletop in the big world within which this is only a toy life. Then the daydream could become anything at all depending upon what was on my mind at the time. The toy world could be under the earth in a forgotten hole out of which I climbed into the real world or it could be on another planet or even in another time.

Sometimes I made it into a contemplative fantasy where the boy/I woke in the night at the wrong time and went out into the artificial world and then suddenly discovered how everything was. For example, he/I stubbed the big toe on the threshold now at the French doors when I ran out into the yard. The whole nail broke. It turned black and the blood ran and grew into a thick scab. I swore. I cursed the threshold which I had been dumb enough to bump. When I did that the threshold disappeared and the French windows changed themselves and fit tight into the floor like a rubber strip instead. Then I began to experiment with various other transformations and discovered little by little that everything around me, the whole house and all the people in it and everything outside, were only a kind of fantasy that becomes solid. If I bothered to fantasize it, they changed again or they dissolved and disappeared and were replaced by something else I fantasized.

That could become a long story too. But the actual discovery was the most interesting. I embroidered it with various details. Since I had happened to find out how things really were, there was not much more to fantasize about. I could just as well light and extinguish suns and be all-powerful, but that didn't produce any interesting fantasies. What was interesting was making the discovery and being astonished.

The other fantasy was different at the beginning. He/I didn't wake up in the middle of the night at the wrong time. There was instead a door. A secret door I was not supposed to know about. Sometimes it was a wallpapered door in my room. With a finger he/I traced the pattern in the wallpaper. It was an ornate pattern with large flowers that opened. Then the secret door suddenly slid open. Without knowing it, he/I had set the mechanism in motion. It opened without a sound. At first I could not see anything beyond it. It was dark. Or, better said, it was as if I had light in my eyes and therefore could not see into the unknown opening.

When I stepped across what I thought was the threshold and came inside, I understood why I could not see. When I came in and turned around I could see that what I had always thought were walls in a house were only painted fabric. I had come to the other side of the curtains. What I had thought was real was only theater. The house was stage scenery. You could get behind it.

I had some difficulty explaining how you could be both behind and in front of the curtains at the same time. Just as one could walk around it, one could come in from behind. I didn't know exactly how that could be done. (It was only later, in New York, when I was eleven or twelve years old and started to read science fiction that I solved the problem with the fourth dimension and such things; but then my fantasy was different.)

I got over the difficulty by telling myself that as long as you stood on the stage or sat in the audience you believed—it looked as if—everything was real. Later, though, when you came through the wallpaper door out into the curtains, you got a look at the machinery.

In any case, I came out and discovered that both the house and what I had believed to be real and Alva and Gunnar and everybody was only theater. Out there was a whole different life. Suddenly the bell rang and everyone rushed to the dressing rooms and took their masks and put on their clothes and went onto the stage and played their roles. You could actually put on any mask you wanted so long as you knew the lines. If the one who played Alva was sick, another could step in and learn the role from the script and put on the Alvamask and Alvaclothes and be Alva in the performance.

I was the only one who walked around being real because I didn't know any better. Now I could let someone else be Jan in that villa while I went out into the world.

Out there I could have different adventures. With a big dog called Käck, I wandered along the roads and slept in barns and in hay if it was summer. We had a lot of experiences. It was different every time. But at Thaliavägen 41 someone else played Jan with a real Jan-mask and everything.

CHAPTER 22

Now I am cycling on Alviksvägen and it is summer. I have come down from Höglandstorget and I am riding fast. The bicycle is new. It is a red Monarch, junior size. The sun is roasting.

Before I even reach Ålstensgatan I hear a car coming up behind me. I pretend to get concerned about the air pressure in the tires. I brake, dismount and feel the front tire with my thumb. I wrinkle my forehead and look thoughtful until the car passes. I am not yet very confident on my bike. But I don't want to let it show. I think it is impolite when cars drive around me and sweep in closely. But I do not want to show that. So I let the drivers see me wonder whether I have a flat tire.

I am going to Solvik Beach. It appears to be very early, because I don't see any other people outside. I see streets and houses and gardens—many of the lawns are yellow from dryness now—and there is Ålsten Forest. But only one car is coming and the streets are deserted. Even the long Ålstensgatan is empty when I look the street.

I pedal hard and bend down over the handlebars and swing off down Solvik Beach Road with a skid so the back wheel squeaks and the whole bike shakes. I put my right foot on the brake with all my strength and the back wheel stops a moment before I let the pedal go and then stomp on it so I really fly down the road toward the beach.

There I go to swimming class. Several of us children lie down and dry swim on the beach. We flap around on command and the teacher blows a whistle. Up and out and then together with the legs, and up and out and together with the legs. The big kids jump at the water's edge a short distance away. They splash water on each other and laugh.

Then we all go down to the dock. Each and every one of us has a life preserver. You have to have it strapped on when you go out on the dock. We climb down the ladder into the water. The swimming teacher stands up on the dock and blows the whistle. Climb down and down and left hand and right and now we are down in the water and float to the left one after the other. When we are all down in the water we are going to practice kicking. We put our legs together and we snort and the swimming teacher blows a tattoo on his whistle and I didn't learn how to swim that summer.

I finally learned in the summer of 1937 when I was ten years old and lived at Kvicksta. I lived in the big house with Folke and Rosina. Stig and Karin lived in the small manager's house. Folke and Stig were my mother's brothers. It was actually Grandfather's farm, but they took care of it for him.

Then, that summer, I went swimming every day. We drove the Ford. It was twelve years old. We used it to take the milk to the dairy at Stallarholm. I had acquired a torn inner tube. If I fixed it I could float on it in the water. I worked for two days to find all the holes. Pump it up. Down into the bucket with the inner tube. Locate the hole. Let the air out. Clean it up. On with the patch and glue it down. The inner tube got to be so good that Folke put it on the Ford when he got a flat tire. Then I fixed the other punctured inner tube to use as a float instead.

The lake where we swam was small. It was behind Björkeby. You drove across the stable yard and walked through the meadow down to the lake. It had clear brown water. Folke and Stig swam and Rosina and Karin sometimes did too, but mostly they sunned themselves. One day Folke said:

"You ought to learn to swim properly. You can't float on the inner tube all the time."

All four of them went out into the water. I was supposed to swim from one to the other in a circle. First we were in such shallow water that my toes hit the bottom when I tried to kick and swim. Then they went further and further out and further and further apart while I swam from one to the other. Finally Folke said when I reached him:

"I can't touch the bottom here either. I'm treading water. Now you can swim."

Then I realized I could swim and I swam every day all that summer. I liked best to swim under water and keep my eyes open just as I reached the bottom and could see the stones fly past me.

But I was still at Solvik Beach, flailing a dry swim, and that must have been the summer of 1935. It is difficult to separate the summers from each other until the summer I was ten years old at Kvicksta.

I stayed mostly with one of my relatives. But sometimes I was at the house on Thaliavägen during the summer. Mary was there and took care of everything. The nurse was in charge of Sissela, and then Kaj after she was born. So there was always some adult to look after me if I was there in the summer.

Alva and Gunnar were away on vacation during the summer. He was on break from the university then. I don't remember whether they ever took Sissela or Kaj with them. I don't think so. I never went along.

They used to travel abroad, I heard. In the fall they gave dinner parties for their friends. I sat in the kitchen with Mary and talked and she gave me some of the roast veal with cream sauce and black currant jelly and ice cream in meringue from their dinner. When Mary served them I heard them talk about their summer vacations. Alva and Gunnar had been in Norway and stayed in a mountain chalet at Myrdal one year. Another year they said they had been in Denmark at the beach and they talked about the dunes and they had been with socialists and artists and psychologists from different countries and had a most interesting time.

In 1937 they went to France. I know that. Because I got a letter from them. It was on my tenth birthday, July 19. "With many greetings from France," they wrote, and enclosed a 100 Franc note with the letter. I was happy. I had never had such a large note before. Because it was my birthday, Stig drove me to Mariefred so I could go to the bank and change the note into Swedish currency. But 100 Francs was not much. If I remember correctly, I got a little more than 14 Crowns. In any case, I went to the kiosk at the bus station and bought ice cream for all of us.

"At least they remembered your birthday," said Stig.

I was down at Tvååker with Gustaf and Mela one summer. That might have been as early as 1934. In any case I didn't have my own bike. Gustaf gave me a lift when we went to the beach. He was church musician in Tvååker then. I was the ringbearer when they got married in Toresund church. I remember he had stepped on a piece of chewing gum. I saw that when he kneeled. It stuck to the sole of his right shoe. I tried to peel it off. His feet spread apart a little, like when you pulled Träff by the small hairs between his toes. Suddenly I noticed that everyone in the church was looking at me. Including the pastor. I had almost got the gum off. Only a few more tugs with the fingernail and it would be free. But I didn't dare continue.

We sang for Gustaf when we were down at the beach. He didn't like to be called a musician and we sang:

"We are musicians, all from Skaraborg..."

It was very shallow. You could go as far out into the sea as you wanted and it still came up just to your stomach. But there was a lot of seaweed in the water and jelly-fish that stung.

While I lived with them at Tvååker I got sick. Gustaf took me to the city and a doctor took my tonsils out with long shiny scissors. It was gruesome.

Fourteen years later Gustaf would play a decisive role in my life. When I met him again in Kristianstad he showed me what artistry was all about. He certainly was a musician. He was a great Swedish composer. But he died young of cancer and when we debated about art and life and duty he had already had one operation and knew that his time was short. He never made any records. But I have a tape from Swedish Radio with one of his compositions. He is played sometimes. But he died before he had a chance to do what he should have done.

I was back at Gesta one summer after we sold the farm. Elon, my mother's brother, was still the leaseholder there. During the day I sat high up in the climbing tree and looked out over the fields as far as the elementary school and the meadows. The wind sang in the birch trees.

I played store with Ulla. She was a few months older and always very orderly. Sometimes I rode a bike across the fields to Ulriksberg and then took the gravel road to Kvicksta, where I got juice and rolls before cycling home again. But I never went up to the big house at Gesta and don't know who lived there.

Then Elon and his family moved north of Lake Mälar. He leased Nibble Farm at Tillberga.

My maternal grandparents lived outside Eskilstuna on the road to Torshälla. The house had an apple orchard in front of it on the road and a big outcropping of rock at the back toward the woods. The summer I lived with them I used to climb up on the rocks and play pirate. The clouds sailed past. Grandfather

Albert took me along when he went out driving. He had a road map beside him on the front seat. You could roll it out. I got to unroll it for him and he drove a long way toward Östergötland and through Närke toward Värmland and the gravel flew up from the wheels onto the fender and he sat quietly almost the whole time. I do not know why he drove so far.

One day when we were driving near Örebro he said suddenly:

"Do you want to drive fast?"

Then we drove 50 miles an hour. I told my paternal grandmother Sofie about that and she got angry and called Grandmother Lowa, but Lowa thought there was no point in talking to Albert because he never answered anyway.

Sometimes we stopped in some village along the way and he treated me to a pastry and juice, but not a soft drink.

"They put uric acid in soft drinks," he said. "That is so people who drink them will get thirsty and buy one more bottle. Juice is better. You know what it is."

Grandmother Lowa mostly stayed upstairs. She was often sick. Sometimes we went out walking, she and I. I got to carry the basket and blanket. When we had passed the houses and reached the clearing she pointed out a good place to sit and we spread out the blanket. She drank coffee and I had juice and we ate cookies and she knitted. Then we went home again.

The living room furniture was black and ornate and polished to a high shine. I don't remember ever using that room. But I used to look in there sometimes. The drapes were drawn closed so the fabric on the sofa would not get faded. It was embroidered with roses. The afternoon sun came in through a gap in the drapes and made the prisms in the chandelier glitter.

There was a large yellow tooth on Grandfather's desk. He said it was a memento. It was his best tooth. He had a box with model houses and I got to play with them. They were from Gemla and they were real houses with balconies and window frames and doors and everything. But everything was so small that you could put it together yourself. You could go into the house if you were smaller than a matchstick.

My paternal grandmother Sofie lived in Mariefred. I stayed there when I was not with one of the other relatives. She was the same as always, only a little older. You had to wash properly and sit properly at the table. She was very careful to have me say my evening prayer.

"Dear God who loves the children dear, watch over me of tender years."

"When you stay with me you do as I tell you and here you say evening prayers."

I don't know where my sisters were during the summer. I never saw them except at the Thaliavägen house. They probably stayed there. I lived there myself in fall 1935 and spring 1936, and fall 1936 and spring 1937. I went to Ålsten School then.

CHAPTER 23

I didn't go to Olovslund School. All the children who lived in Olovslund went there, except the ones who attended private schools in town. I went to Ålsten School. I took the streetcar there. The number 12 came from Nockeby past Nockeby Square and when it got to Olovslund I got on. After that came Högland Square and Ålsten Yard where there was a turnaround for the 12A, which didn't go any further, and then came Ålsten Street and there I got off.

Prime Minister Per Albin lived down the street, but I went the other way toward the school. It was big and yellow and built in a corner way up the street. Ålsten Street ended there.

I was supposed to learn how to manage money, so I didn't have a streetcar pass, but had to buy tickets. That took a large part of my allowance. It was like having to pay to go to school, even if it wasn't much. Because of that, I got good at riding free. I used to stand toward the back end and disappear. I made myself invisible and the conductor didn't notice I was there. When he called out to ask whether anyone had got on, I didn't hear. On the way up to school there was a discount store where you could pay with streetcar tickets. You didn't get as much as when you paid with money. The lady in the store took five öre per ticket for the effort of cashing them, she said. Someone squealed on her and the police questioned her and the chance to shop with streetcar tickets was over. But that was not until 1937, I think.

The reason I had to go to Ålsten School and didn't get to go to Olovslund School was that I was a problem child. At Ålsten School there was a teacher who could handle problem children.

They told me that and I was suspicious from the beginning.

I came in the door and gave my name and all the children looked at me. They had already been in the class for a year.

"I'm supposed to join your class," I said.

"That's nice," she said.

Then I had to sit at a desk by the inside wall.

She had white hair and her name was Miss Rehn. She was a very good teacher. I didn't think she was different from the others and couldn't see how she was especially qualified to teach problem children and she didn't treat me in a special way either. She treated us all alike.

Sometimes we did fun things. We had a schoolyard and we made potato flour. We wrote and my handwriting was ugly. We had arithmetic and lessons in Christianity and then pictures of Jesus were hung on the wall.

The only report card I still have from my childhood is from second grade. It doesn't say much. They didn't give particularly high grades in elementary school. The highest I had was B+. That was nothing special, even if high grades were seldom given. Otherwise they were B or B-.

One thing I could do was read aloud. I could do that better than anyone in the class. I could do that better than the teacher herself. All the others read from the book and you could tell that even if they didn't stumble and hesitate over the words. But I could take the words and let them come as if they were being spoken by someone else. I could let words come at the same time as I looked at what was coming next, and I could get the whole thing to flow smoothly. I could even turn pages without anyone noticing it in the way I read. I liked to read aloud. I used to read aloud for myself when I was alone or tell stories and take on many voices which could sound altogether different.

Because of this I didn't get to read particularly often. On only a few occasions when something had to be read aloud and she didn't want to read herself, I got to come forward and read. Otherwise I sat and listened to the others who chopped and stumbled and could not read a whole page at a time, but read letter by letter and word by word.

Mostly I didn't listen. I tuned out. If it was a new book I read on ahead of the class. I read fast and didn't need to move my lips or whisper like the others.

The library was located in the school building. There was just a separate entrance. Miss Rehn took us to the library and there we learned how to find books. But we were allowed only in the children's room. You could borrow two fun books at a time. The others had to be non-fiction. But the fun books were not particularly fun and it took a while before I could borrow for real.

When we got to play shipwreck and climb ropes and things, gym class was fun. Otherwise I didn't like it. To jump in place or run in a circle around the room or wave your arms didn't amuse me. For the most part I didn't bother to do it. They tried to talk me into it, but in the end they gave up and let me be. I was surprised the others never did as they wanted but only did as they were told.

I hardly ever went around with anyone in my class. They lived far away in Bromma and we only saw each other during school time. But there were several I talked to and played with and liked. It became a problem when we began playing rounders and handball and other such games.

I knew about soccer and such things. I had watched real soccer too. Uncle Gösta, who had been on the national team, took me along to soccer games sometimes. Afternoons and Sundays children used to gather at various places around

Bromma and kick at a ball. They did that on Kungsholmen too. But I had never bothered to go there myself.

When I played in the schoolyard and the teacher divided us into two teams, I knew the rules. But I didn't like them and didn't follow them. I played with my friends instead. It didn't matter to me that they were on the opposing team. The teacher blew her whistle and everyone screamed and yelled and wondered whether I knew how to play. I said I knew how to play, but wanted to do it my own way. They gradually began to play their game again and I sat on the sidelines and was supposed to watch, but thought about something else.

For the most part the days went by as usual in school and one day was like another. Now I can't distinguish days, weeks, months or even years from each other. They were all alike. Miss Rehn was nice and there were no conflicts and my grades never rose above B+.

Two fantasies belong to the school years from fall 1935 though spring 1937. Rather, there were two fantasy systems. They are a little hard to describe because I came across them in reading later in spring 1939, when I had changed languages, lived in New York and was an American. But they belong to this time.

One is flying. I sit on my bench and the sun shines through the drapes and there is a murmur around me. The hour has just begun and there is a lot left of the morning. No one sees as I carefully free myself from the bench. With a few light hand movements I am up. Everything is still and flying is actually natural. All people can do it, if they only knew they could will it. When I am so high no one can see me, even if they stood on the toes and stretched themselves, the class discovers what I have done. They point at me and call to each other, but I don't hear them because I am flying. I can only see them make faces and watch their mouths gape. Teacher slams her book on the lectern, but not a sound can be heard up here. I sail slowly toward the window and it opens. Outside it is summer and green and I hear the birds. Now I glide out through the open window. Outside the sky is deep blue and the clouds float away above the birches and disappear from Ålsten School.

The daydream is no longer than that. I backed up and began again in a new way and did other things. Sometimes I flew past other classroom windows and looked into them. Sometimes I flew round and round above the schoolyard during recess. Everyone pointed at me and the teachers came with those sticks with a hook used for putting up maps. They tried to hook me with them and pull me down. I teased them and flew close, close, close, but always just out of their reach.

That was a fun dream and you could do a lot with different things.

Sometimes they caught me as I sat and dreamed about flying. Then they asked what I was thinking about and I wasn't startled or anything. I just lied because I didn't want to be sullen and said:

"Nothing."

In spring 1939 I discovered that Booth Tarkington wrote almost the same daydream in *Penrod*. It was a good book. Many times better than all the "William" books, but the same kind of thing. Only in Penrod's daydream he was caught. They got hold of him by calling him down. When I read Tarkington I had already stopped dreaming the flying dream for good. I only remember that I used to dream it. In 1939 it was the invisibility dream.

The other daydream was one I could not dream in school. There were too many children around and they disturbed the dreaming. I dreamed this one as I walked down to the streetcar stop, or when I stood waiting, or when I could be completely left alone without anyone coming and taking me away or calling to me or talking to me. It was the dream about the other world.

There had always been images in front of me when I closed my eyes. Especially when I was tired, the pictures came closer. There were faces and people and animals and even landscapes. They still come. To some extent they can be controlled. I see a face and it begins to change and change. I can see it distorted. Take it at an angle. But it is not always possible to control. It is usually a surging image. There is no need to be concerned about it. It is like that with music and voices.

Maybe I ought to say there were never voices from outside nor images which pretended to be real. I never had any trouble orienting myself and knowing what was real. It is the same for everyone, if they listen and look. Yes, it is the same for my dogs too. That is why they can dream and jump in their sleep and yelp and twitch and their fur stands up. They are extremely dramatic in their dog dreams. You can get certain dogs to see things when they are awake too. You can sit and play and pretend with a dog that way. I used to sit with Träff like that at Kvicksta.

With a little will, a musical fragment can become a whole long piece. The various phrases of music which pop up and cut away like ice floes in a stream, can be gathered into long conversations.

That other fantasy was rather complicated. It was as if two worlds existed. One world was real in the usual way and in the other I saw images and heard music and speech. It was as if I could create this world just by thinking of it like this. Later I thought this other world was ordinary and real, and the one with Ålsten School was only images and fragments of speech swirling out. When I concentrated on it I could begin the day-dream.

This other world was often located in another place. I often placed it in the South Seas or in Africa because I had fantasized a lot about Africa when I went to Olof's School. I had my eyes and ears in the other world even though I breathed in this one. When I touched myself in this world I touched myself in the same way in the other one. I let the images and sounds become everything.

I walked down Ålstensgatan toward the streetcar stop and in the other world I was on an island in the South Seas with palms and sand. There were not the same hills in both worlds. Sometimes it was like walking on air in the other world when I walked on a street in this one. Sometimes it was like walking underground in the other world when I walked on a street in this one and I went straight out into the blue lagoon and sank deeper and deeper into the clear water with all the fish around me and I walked down to the number 12 stop.

This dream could also be created in many ways.

In spring 1939 in New York I read *The Remarkable Case of Davidson's Eyes* by H.G. Wells and was astonished. But he used a lot of apparatus and a whole explosion to create his dream. He only saw. He didn't hear and couldn't move back and forth.

I assumed that Wells had the same kind of daydreams and he had used them and written them out for the public. Then he had to back them up with explanations to avoid unnecessary questions. By that time I was no longer in the South Seas. Instead I went around Europe where there was going to be war or I was in outer space which I had read about in *Astounding*.

CHAPTER 24

It was the day Lappland crashed. I had been up in the climbing tree with Olle and Lennart and we were building a hut. The evening air was transparently clear. The sky was green and from the highest branch of the climbing tree you could look far out over houses and groves.

We had been talking about Lappland. Olle thought it was the pilot's fault. He should not have given it so much gas before he got up high. I thought the Fokker plane was probably not as safe as they said. It was past noon and getting on toward evening. We slipped down from the treehouse we had built up high in the pine. The trunk was smooth and it was hard to climb up. That was why we were left alone with our treehouse.

Olle went home and I went toward Thaliavägen 41. I had hurt my right big toe. It was bloody. The nail was beginning to come off again. I used to bang up my toe at the beginning of the summer and then stub it a little from time to time. That could not be helped. I had resin on my shirt too. It was still sticky and I tried to peel it off so they would not see, but it turned into a big stain instead.

When I got home Gunnar and Rolf Bergman were sitting at the table in the yard. Gunnar was drinking cherry liqueur from the silver cup Grandfather gave me when I was baptized. I tried to get past them but Gunnar called to me. I had to go say hello.

"Look at what a fatty he's become," said Gunnar. Rolf Bergman said nothing. He just nodded.

Gunnar patted me on the stomach.

"Are you going to give birth soon?" he said. "You must be in your ninth month by now." Then he laughed. Rolf Bergman said nothing. He just nodded.

Yes, I had grown fat. That is what they told me and I knew it was true.

"Doesn't your rear end shake when you walk?" said Gunnar.

There was no way to answer. It was best to pretend you had heard nothing when he said things like that. Mary came with juice for me and I sat down a short distance from them.

"You just eat your roll," said Gunnar and laughed again.

Rolf Bergman was one of Gunnar's friends from student days. He was a little older than Gunnar. Doctors used to play a lot of practical jokes in those days. They stuffed body parts into their pockets when they left class and played jokes on people. They pulled a hand out of a pocket when they were about to shake hands and people jumped. That was amusing, said Gunnar. One time someone took a whole thighbone and laid it in the bed of a theologian from Enköping. He had a room on Odenplan. When he got into bed that night and found the bone there he was beside himself. He just sat and rolled his eyes. When Gunnar was in the mood he used to talk about such things.

Now Rolf Bergman was talking about a girl who lived in the house. She was from the country and had only been in Stockholm a short time.

"I got suspicious of her so I called her in and examined her more closely and found she had gonorrhea."

Gunnar and Rolf laughed and then Gunnar caught sight of me again.

"How are you doing, Joe?" he said.

I knew I was fat. I could see it in the mirror. I had been fat for more than a year now. I detested it. Gunnar despised fat people. His sisters were fat too. He teased them too. Sometimes he made them cry. But I didn't cry. I just smiled.

"He's just like Mr. Wardle's Fat Joe," said Gunnar. "He just sits there and dozes as if there was no life in him."

"Hey, Joe, wake up!" said Gunnar and reached out his hand to pat me on the stomach.

"I'm not sleeping," I said.

Gunnar never got tired of making jokes about Joe. He thought it was especially funny to get hold of me when guests were there. I could barely read Dickens. I used to skip the chapter where Joe comes in when I read the book about Pickwick. Grandfather had bought it and I read it at Grandmother's house in Mariefred. But I skipped that chapter at the beginning where Joe just eats and sleeps and dozes as soon as he sits down.

"It's perfectly normal that the fat boy in Dickens should sleep," said Rolf Bergman. "They do that. It has to do with lack of oxygen. There are some patients who can't stay awake if they happen to sit down. The diaphragm presses on the lungs and and they fall asleep. It's almost like a pilot having a black-out."

The evening was still quiet and transparently clear. The sky was a bottle green and the pines black silhouettes. Here there were mountains at the horizon. The table and chairs stood on solid rock. I looked at them and made them small, as if seeing them through the wrong end of a telescope. Then I stepped on my secret pedal and now the hole opened and Gunnar and Rolf disappeared into the underworld with a terrible roar. The hatch opened when I stepped on that secret pedal.

There was a huge room down there. But I could see them clearly. The flames fluttered around them and roasted them on a spit. They were alive the whole time. They flailed and fought and everything sizzled around them.

I could see their eyes. They were wide open. But I just smiled at them and thought about the secret pedal again and now the hatch slid back noiselessly and there was only a murmur in the treetops and a bird far away. I was alone in the yard. High up in the bottle-green sky appeared a black flying machine on its way north. It was high up and I stood up and watched it a long time and then called as loud as I dared:

"Come on, new Lappland! Come on, new Lappland!"

CHAPTER 25

WE LOOK AT OUR HOME TOWN.

Our school building is 315 feet long and 32 feet wide. Our classroom is 26 feet long and 21 feet 6 inches wide. We have three windows facing the schoolyard and two doors to the corridor. We have two cabinets, a chair and desk for the teacher, and thirty-one school desks.

Ålsten School is new. We have 20 classrooms, two gyms, one sewing room, one handcraft room, one physics lab, one auditorium, library, mailroom, dental office, swimming pool, kitchen, two teacher lounges, four supply rooms with storerooms, boiler room and laundry. In addition there are living quarters for the custodian and cleaning woman. Then we left the school building.

First we went into the school garden. There we would look at flowers. We saw marigolds, mignonettes, asters, sunflowers, columbines, cock's combs. Then we saw oaks, red currants, black currants, gooseberries. And we saw corn, hemp. Then we went on an excursion.

When we went out on this excursion we gathered in the schoolyard to leave. First we walked Ålstensgatan and then Bergviksvägen until we came to the steps leading to Storskogen. On the mountain we saw long grooves in the rock from the ice age and crevices. We also saw big boulders which the ice had dragged along in those days. Below the mountain there were marshy places with sedge. Then we went up a hill and came to a Viking grave at the very top. Then we went on to an overlook and saw Lake Mälar with bays and sounds and

fjords and islands and islets and peninsulas and points.
Then we took Bergviksvägen again and saw a boat yard. At Alviksvägen we saw tennis courts. Mälar Park lay beside the lake. We saw Vasterbro in the distance and then we went on and saw Bergsund shipyard the mechanical workshop above it. Then we went on and came to Solvik Bridge and from there we saw Högalid Church and Storkyrkan and the German Church. Then we saw King's Hat. We came to the big ski jumping tower at the very end. The weather was good.

Jan Myrdal
Third Grade

CHAPTER 26

Monday, September 28, 1936, I was on the kitchen floor reading *Svenska Dagbladet*. Mary thought I was in the way and kept after me until I crept under the table with my newspaper. When I looked up I could see her legs wander back and forth. She was setting the table for us in the kitchen. We were having hash. Alva and Gunnar didn't eat hash. They ate meat with green salad later.

The hash was actually hashed tripe. I knew that. When I was small I ate neither tripe nor blood sausage, but I ate hash and black sausage. One day when I was shopping with Mary at the butcher's on the square, she asked for a pound of tripe and a pound of blood pudding for the child. I protested.

"You know I don't eat tripe or blood pudding," I said.

"You've been eating tripe and blood pudding all your life," she said. "They have just been calling it something else.

We had a new government in Sweden. Gunnar was not appointed to a position in it. Per Albin had broken with the Peasant Party. In Spain the war was going badly. *Svenska Dagbladet* wrote that the Reds had fled and Cordoba was liberated. Alcazar's heroic defenders had been rescued, wrote *Svenska Dagbladet*. It was a Right-wing paper. I didn't usually read it. I read the *Social Democrat*. But now *Svenska Dagbladet* had a picture of me. I was there right under the names of the members of the new government and beside the news from the war.

In the picture I was wearing a trenchcoat and cap. It was still summer so I had not started wearing knickers yet, but was still in shorts. My socks had fallen down and I had on sandals instead of shoes. But I was not alone in the picture. Someone else stood beside me. We were the same height. He was wearing a trenchcoat too, but his trenchcoat was blue and mine was gray. He had shoes and knickers and a shirt with a tie. Our faces didn't show. We were in profile and turned so only our right ears were visible.

Svenska Dagbladet wrote that they were "two young Messrs. Myrdal." Many thought the picture was of me and my brother. They talked about that brother for a long time. One summer day in 1965 I had lunch at Freden. One of my teachers from Högland School in 1943 came in. Someone pointed me out to him. He came over to my table.

"I had your brother in my class," he said. "Your older brother. How is he doing these days?"

He told me about his troubles with my older brother. He waited for me to ask him to sit at my table. I didn't do that. I didn't see him. He didn't exist. After a while he cleared his throat and said:

"I'd better go back to my own table."

"Did you see they think Olle is my brother?" I said to Mary.

It was Olle who stood next to me in the *Svenska Dagbladet* picture. We had gone to the dedication of a new section of Kristineberg. Markelius had designed the houses. They were houses for large families. Later they came to be called Myrdal Houses.

Houses for large families were shown on Sunday for members of the city council and other interested persons. Among the visitors were two young Messrs. Myrdal, who appear here in this picture beside two new houses in the Kristineberg area.

In the picture I am standing reading plans and Olle is holding open a door. Seven years later I often went through that door and up the stairway because Tore Forsberg lived there. We were together a lot at the end of the war and he became chairman of the club in which I was study leader. Now he is party secretary for the Party of the Left, Communist and it has been several years since we last met.

Then, that Sunday at the end of September 1936 when the houses were shown, Olle and I had taken the streetcar to Kristineberg because were were interested in houses and housing construction. In my room I had a lot of books with pictures of new areas in Vienna and Hamburg and other places. I used to draw plans myself too. It was fun to calculate where the windows should be and which way the doors should open and how you could go from room to room. That was why I took Olle along to Kristineberg.

Gotthard Johansson was not terribly fond of the plans, I remember, and I had agreed with him when I was under the kitchen table. If people were going to move there because they were crowded at home and had a lot of children, but then had to live with five people in one room and a kitchen, it was not especially good. The bathroom in the basement was not good either. Everything was narrow and small. But Markelius was a good designer, I thought. His house was interesting. Next to model planes and steam engines, I was most interested in building houses at those days.

Svenska Dagbladet's photographer had discovered us while I stood reading plans and talked with Olle about what was wrong with the designs.

Olle and his brother Lennart, who was one year younger, were my best friends and we used to get together every day. Only they went to Olovslund School and I went to Ålsten

School.

In the evenings we climbed buildings out at Nockeby. They were building villas there. We jumped on the beams and balanced high up on the rafters. Then we took nails and boards for our treehouse. Such things were everywhere on the construction site and no one noticed that we took just a few.

We talked about building a big hut in the woods but never did it. We would not have been able to keep it. The bigger boys would just take it if it turned out well. We didn't want to build on Olle and Lennart's property either. Their parents would ask where we got the boards and nails and there would have to be a lot of explanations and things. If we built on the property at Thaliavägen 41, Mary would notice what we were doing and she and the nurse would ask. That was why we built the treehouse up in the pine. None of the grownups could get up there and the big boys didn't bother to climb up there.

The pine was tall. It was pretty difficult to get up it. You had to climb the same way you climbed lampposts and telephone poles. Hold your legs together and struggle up. Once you were up a few feet it went better. There were stumps of branches to hold and then branches and at the top there was a lot of space.

We began by nailing beams between the branches to make a good foundation for the floor. Then we nailed down a floor so all three of us could sit. Once in a while someone else got to come along too. Five of us could crowd together up there. It shook and creaked, but it held. We talked about making walls and a roof as well, but that was more difficult. There were no good places to fasten them. We chopped large pine branches with Olle's scout axe and wove walls and a roof from them. From the ground, you could hardly see our treehouse and when you saw it you almost thought it could be a big bird's nest.

You had to be careful coming down. Otherwise you could get caught on one of the dry branches. That happened to me once. A small stump of a branch gouged my thigh. It hurt and there I sat. It had gone in deep. It took me a while to get loose. Both Olle and Lennart pulled me and I kicked with all my might and came loose and fell down. It was not really very high, only a few feet and it didn't matter. But the blood ran down my leg and it throbbed.

When I got to Thaliavägen 41 I cleaned myself as best I could in the rainwater barrel outside so no one would notice I was bleeding Then I went up to my room and bandaged myself with the old nightshirt I had used as a Star Boy at the Lucia Fest in school. It was lumpy and messy, but not much blood got on my bed. The next day it was all dry but the leg had swollen and it throbbed and I had some difficulty walking for a while. No one noticed anything and I avoided questions. The scar is still there. It is large and located on the inside of my right thigh. It looks as if someone stuck a bayonette in me. In later years girls used to ask what it was.

"Nothing," I used to say.

We were not at Thaliavägen 41 very much. Most often we were in Olle and Lennart's room. They had a big room with beds on top of each other like in a sleeping car. Olle slept in the upper bunk and there was a wooden ladder.

We built things with their Meccano and their father had brought new toys from Germany. They had soldiers who were not pewter soldiers, but made of some synthetic material and painted real colors. The soldiers had cannons and a field kitchen and everything they needed. There was also a fine heavy Mercedes convertible with rubber wheels. You could steer it. With that there was a Hitler who stood up and greeted the people and twelve SS men. That way you could have Hitler drive past his soldiers and greet them. Olle and Lennart's father admired Hitler for what he did for Germany. When Olle told him what I said about Hitler he thought the boys shouldn't listen to such talk. But he didn't forbid them to play with me. Just the opposite. He said Olle was big enough now to take the train to Germany in the summer and he could take me along. At first I was going to go, but then Grandmother said it wasn't a good idea and I went to Mariefred instead.

When Bromma Airport opened we were there. We had cycled there, all three of us, and watched as airplanes gave a demonstration. There were a lot of people out there. The king had been there too, but we didn't see him. At the exhibition we saw the big modern planes. Olle showed me a Junkers "Ju 86" and said with a plane like that the Germans could either win a war or control the whole world's air traffic.

When we sat up in the treehouse in the pine and looked out over Bromma, we talked about flights we had made all over the world. Time after time we flew over the Atlantic and Pacific Oceans. Sometimes we crashed, but escaped after great adventures. We overcame all difficulties. When we had engine failure over the middle of the Atlantic we let the controls go and pulled down our flight goggles so the wind wouldn't blind us. We opened the hatch and climbed out to the engine. It roared and oil sprayed our faces. All the time we held on with our left hands and hung by our knees as we repaired the engine with the big wrench we had carried in our mouths up from the cockpit. Now as we worked on the engine we noticed the plane had lost power and then it stalled and then began to spin toward the stormy sea below us. It whistled and roared and oil sprayed, but calm and coldblooded, we kept working on the engine until it was fixed. Then we climbed back into the cockpit again without hurrying because we saw it was still 1192 feet to the waves. When we had returned to our seats and taken control of the plane we pulled it up out of its spin. The plane shook as it rose and swept so close to the boiling storm-whipped white-caps that salt spray swirled against the windshield. With a roaring engine and racing propeller we climbed higher and higher toward the sky, which was bright blue, almost black.

CHAPTER 27

Mary must have been off that afternoon because Alva came into the kitchen and I didn't get the refrigerator door closed before she was standing behind me watching. I had taken a meatball from the yellow bowl in the refrigerator. It was supposed to be for dinner. Now a hole showed where the meatball had been. It was shiny as an oozing sore in the mass of meatballs.

"If you're going to do things you're not supposed to, you must make sure no one catches you," said Alva.

"If you steal meatballs you have to do it so no one sees you. You have to rearrange the meatballs so there won't be a hole."

She rearranged the meatballs so no one could see I had taken one.

"Take another meatball," she said.

I did. But it didn't taste good. It was like eating sawdust.

"Now move them," she said.

I moved the meatballs around.

"It shouldn't look too perfect," said Alva. "It has to look like it did before and give the impression the meatballs have just been put into the bowl from the frying pan."

She patted several of the meatballs so they broke the symmetry I had built up.

"Like this," she said. "Now it looks natural. Now no one can see that you took meatballs without permission."

She took a glass down from the shelf, filled it with water, and left. I stood there in the kitchen. Now the meatball taste was a cold and greasy film in my mouth. I went to the sink and spat. Then I stuck my right index finger and middle finger down my throat and threw up the meatballs. A sour, ill-smelling sludge burned my throat. I ran water and washed the vomit down the drain. I rinsed until everything was gone. I looked myself over carefully so no one could see what I had done. I washed my mouth with water time after time and sniffed to see whether anyone could smell that I had vomited. Everything was as it should be and nothing showed and no one could smell anything either. It was still afternoon and a long time until evening and I went out.

Whatever you did it was important not to leave traces. It was just as important to have clean underpants in case you got run over and ended up in the hospital. Someone else would see you had shit on your underpants.

Everything had to look right. If you did something that wasn't right you had to do it so it wouldn't show. You had to use the correct words too when others could hear. You always had to remember that someone could hear you.

Alva was always afraid that Gunnar would misspeak when people could hear him. She trembled when he said:

"What a Jew!"

She looked tormented when Gunnar went in through a door marked "No Entrance" and he said:

"No prohibitions apply to Gunnar Myrdal!"

But he didn't say things like that when others were listening. You had to watch your tongue. It was like saying "maid." That was never done when a housekeeper was listening.

Alva saw to it that nothing inappropriate was said.

"Gunnar, dear," she said. "Gunnar, dear." Then she switched from Swedish to English. "Not in front of the servants and children." She was chirping when she said that. Then she smiled. They spoke English when I was in the vicinity. Later they began to suspect that I understood and they switched to French. But

Gunnar was not as good at that. He answered only with single
syllables and grunted.

Alva had a special way of chirping when someone said
something that would not be appropriate for others to hear. In
taxis and on the streetcar and on the train and at the movies it
was always best to be quiet. You never knew who was listening. You could talk about the weather or chocolate cookies or
something. That was especially important when you were with
friends. You never knew what kind of parents they had.

I got an allowance. It was supposed to cover all my daily
expenses. That was why I learned to ride free on the streetcar.
I worked for additional money. Each chore had its price.
Mowing the lawn was 25 öre. Digging in the ground was 30
öre. Running errands was ten öre if it was just going to and
from Percy Luck at Höglandstorget or to the bakery. But it could
go up to 25 öre, or even more if it was a complicated assign-
ment.

I didn't get this money at once. Alva wrote it down in a little notebook with black covers. If there was something I really
wanted to buy, the money was added up. If what I wanted to
buy was worthwhile and educational, then she added an equal
amount. If my assets were not large enough so that doubling
sufficed, she became very secretive and sat with the black book
in front of her and erased and wrote and erased and wrote.
Finally she got the calculations to work and I could buy whatever it was. But it was always just as awful and suspenseful until
you knew what she would do.

I loathed it.

But I learned to calculate in the same way. When I did
errands and was supposed to shop I took a rubber eraser and
pencil and on the way home I changed the receipts. I didn't
take much. No one would know. I didn't need so much that

anyone would wonder and begIn to ask questions and if anyone asked it would be such a small alteration that the shop
would not be sure whether it was a mistake. Only a few öre
here and there and see that it all added up. It was like slicing
off a few shavings.

I practiced a long time to make the alterations undetectable.
It was a matter of erasing correctly. You had to be careful the
shop didn't use an indelible pencil. The figures had to be made
correctly too. And you couldn't press too hard. Now I always
kept receipts in my pocket, so they were used to them being a
little dirty and crumpled. That made it easier to change the
receipts without anyone noticing. I also had to add very carefully so everything came out right.

With money I got that way I could buy Sport Cola and
Pirate Gum and lots of other things.

Alva kept books on everything in the house. What all the
different children cost. Everything guests ate. Everything that
was bought. She filled different notebooks with columns of figures. She thought that was amusing. She could sit by herself
and write figures and calculate. But she didn't do that only for
our household. She kept books on the whole family. Everyone
owed Gunnar and Alva money. I understood that by the time I
was about ten. It had to do with Grandfather's death. Alva had
worked out how Grandmother could live as usual and everyone
would pay for it as if Grandfather had left her money. Because
there was no such money the brothers and sisters would pay.
But because they had had different opportunities and were to
pay what they had cost Grandfather in education and other
things, it was Gunnar who paid and then the brothers and sisters were to pay Gunnar according to Alva's calculations. It was
a very intricate system. No one in the family understood it
except Alva.

Ten years later when I sat with Gustaf Carlman at the Freemason Hotel in Kristianstad and he invited me to a smorgaasbord, wormwood akvavit and beer, he said:

"If I buy you a drink I don't immediately write it up in some book. I don't go along with that Myrdal bookkeeping. I won't have anything to do with it. If she says we owe money, I agree. If she says we don't owe money, I agree with that too. There are too many other things to do in life than count money and keep books."

I told him what it was like and how I had to calculate and falsify and embezzle and erase and write and erase again so the whole thing would come out right. He said:

"Forget it. You don't owe them a justification. You didn't ask to be born. Parents are responsible for taking care of their offspring when they bring them into the world. You've got to understand that you're not the one who's crazy."

That was beautiful. Gustaf laughed and put herring with potatoes on his plate. He lifted the akvavit glass and said:

"Skål!"

I still can't count money. I stick my hand down into my pocket and feel whether there are any coins there. I take a look in my wallet. When I am supposed to keep books I get a rash on my hands and feel nauseous from uneasiness. In front of me I see again my childhood's hellish columns of numbers and falsified receipts that always threatened some small error here or there and risked discovery.

It is possible that it is like that in other situations and other families. But I have never come in contact with a family where this multiple bookkeeping was so ingrained in the system and where there were so many commonplace things you were not allowed to mention and in which you had to watch your tongue.

It continues in the households of my sisters. My younger sister Kaj is married and lives in Germany. She lives in Göttingen. I had liked her. In 1970 when we drove the car back from India we got off the highway and visited. My niece Nicky looked at me with big eyes and said:

"But Mom, do you have a brother?"

Kaj was embarrassed and laughed. She said there had not been much occasion to speak of me.

She had married twelve years earlier. That was in India. We had been there. Afterward, when she was waiting to leave for Europe, she sat and talked about the whole cobweb of book-keeping in the family and how Alva kept books and made entries and deletions and erased and corrected. Finally she broke into tears.

"I never want to be like that," she said. "Never."

Though she was only a girl, Nicky was one of Gunnar's favorite grandchildren. In that case there probably was no occasion to mention me. It was—as Gustaf used to say—a Myrdal situation through and through.

Words were a game. Gestures, tones and movements were signs. When you learned the rules, the game was not incomprehensible. It was just different from other families.

I thought about the last time I saw Alva. It was the fall of 1967. She was Minister for Disarmament. It must have been August or September. She called suddenly and invited Gun and me to dinner. She took us to the Aurora. It was the only time we ever went to that restaurant. She was never stingy when she really invited someone. It was always been pleasant to shop with her for clothes and jewelry and antiques. She was always charming to talk to. She was justly known for that.

I could tell she wanted something, but I didn't know what. I assumed she would get to it eventually. Meanwhile we ate well and drank a good bottle of wine and chatted.

Suddenly she laughed. It was a high, piercing laugh. I could see it coming now.

"Erlander wondered if we get together. He was concerned about that. I have to be loyal to my colleagues. It might be best if we didn't see each other for a while."

Then she laughed her piercing laugh again and said "Skål." She was in the government then. Tage Erlander was prime minister. I was active in the movement for solidarity with the people of Vietnam and had just come back from Cambodia. I had also spoken for the rights of Palestinians after the Six Day War. I had publicly opposed the Swedish government's foreign policy in my writing for the social democratic press.

"Yes, that probably is best," I said.

Driving home, Gun's lips were pale with rage.

"She can just go eat her Sunday dinner with Erlander from now on," she said.

We used to see Alva and Gunnar several times a year. Gunnar, of course, would quarrel first and then fall asleep. I was used to that from childhood. We didn't have many relatives in the older generation. It was only right to visit them sometimes. Now we had been freed from that duty.

"You don't really believe it was Erlander who said anything about Alva seeing me," I said. "You don't really believe Erlander warned her about seeing her own children?"

"But Alva said..."

"Erlander is no brilliant politician or great thinker," I said. "He's just an ordinary man with an ordinary family life. It would never occur to him to ask Alva, whom he sees as my mother, to stop seeing me for the sake of the party. What she said about Erlander was just an excuse. She erased a little bit in the books so it would look better. She concluded on her own that it would be poor tactics to see me. She's afraid that she won't get to be foreign minister if people think we're close.

"That was what she was signaling with her laugh. She always laughs like that in such situations. She's done that as long as I can remember."

I was not particularly hurt or upset that evening at the Aurora. Gun was only because she had not grown up in the family. I took Alva at her word. She had now said what she had to say.

I knew what a double-thinker she was. Rather, I knew what a crooked thinker she was. I also knew that she had no idea how much I knew. Since 1955 I had known what she reported about me to the United States immigration authorities. She was stopped and questioned and she informed on me on her arrival in New York in the summer of 1953. There was no need. She had diplomatic immunity. She just collaborated. I prefer the way Gunnar handled such things. When McCarthy sent his boys to the United Nations in Geneva to investigate the Economic Commission for Europe, for which Gunnar was the general secretary, he kicked them out. But Alva did not. Alva's secretary at UNESCO was so shocked that she told me in detail when I came to Paris in July 1955. But I had said nothing to Alva.

Now I took her at her word.

"You say Erlander is concerned," I said. "Yes, then it is probably best we don't ever see each other again."

CHAPTER 28

In a book of local Bromma history I see I was mistaken. We didn't fight. We were not cruel.

But we did fight. And we were cruel. I was only ten, so I was among the youngest. But I was there when the leaders executed enemy spies. They were tied to a tree and we shot salt pellets into their rear ends with air rifles and air guns. They yelled.

We broke into Rag-Nicke's barn to steal helmets and sabres. There were some in his storage shed. The leaders sat outside at the ditch and kept watch and I and the other younger ones were sent across the plank. It was easy to break the door open. It wasn't even padlocked. But there were only enough helmets and sabres for the leaders.

I heard about other fights in the city. All the neighborhoods fought each other. It was dangerous to leave your own neighborhood. You could get caught. In Kungsholmsstrand I heard they got hold of the leader of the gang which controlled the other end of the bridge. He had walked Alströmergatan all alone one afternoon. They took him and beat him until he told them he was going to visit an aunt. Then they tied him so he couldn't escape and took him to the grove. One of the boys ran home and got a bucket. Then they all pissed in the bucket. There were twenty of them now, so the bucket got really full. Then they lashed the gang leader to a pine and emptied the bucket over him slowly. It was sunny and broiling and he was soaked through and stank. Then they took the bucket and left him and he had to stand there in the broiling sun all day until some ladies came by. At first they thought he was playing. Then they untied him.

I was a member of several gangs. I was good at fighting too. I could shut out the pain when I was hit. It didn't hurt as it did for most others. I would go first. I swung a stick around me. It was heavy. It could crush the skull of anyone who came too close. Then I yelled and ran away. That was why they called me the Saber Swinger.

When I heard them talk about me and say, "Go for it, Saber Swinger!" I was proud. But I often took a beating. I was just one of the younger ones.

One time someone hit me over the head with a plank. The kid was probably twelve or thirteen years old. He had run into a building. We blocked the exits and he was caught. He was trapped in a corner. Then he picked up a plank and banged it on my head before I could get away. Then it all got black and red and heavy and I almost fell over but managed to stay on my feet. All I could see was something like a small hole in the middle of the blackness. They all cheered and screamed with joy even though the kid got away because the plank broke and he ran off. I assume it was rotten. Or maybe there was a big knot in the wood.

"Stoneskull!"

"Stoneskull!" they yelled.

I felt a little sick and wanted to vomit. But I didn't show it. We sat on the slope above Västerled. The leaders smoked and asked me if I wanted a drag too.

One of the leaders—he had red hair and lived by Olovslund School—told how his father had smuggled a whole sugar carton of Nick Carter books when they were forbidden. There were up in the attic.

"They're great books," he said. "There are corpses under floors and secret doors and detectives shoot people right in the face."

I thought about those books a lot after that. They had been forbidden because there was too much murder in them. I would have liked to read them, but it was impossible.

I sat up front at the movies. The seats beside me and right behind me were empty. I was always by myself in the first row. Back where all the kids sat I couldn't see what was happening on the screen. Others could read signs from across the street and go to the movies and sit in about the tenth row. I could not do that. In school it was always difficult to read what the teacher wrote on the blackboard. But for the most part I could guess. To know whether it was ten thousand or a hundred thousand in numbers I had to pick off the zeros and count them one at a time. If I just looked at them they jumped back and forth and it was impossible to know whether it was four or five zeros in a row. It was as if they jumped around on the line.

That was why I sat in the first row when I was sent to the movies. The figures were large and powerful in front of me and I had to tilt my head back to see them properly. The loudspeakers rumbled in front of me and horses' hooves clattered. The black rider came toward me and shot bam, bam, bam. Enemies fell dead from their horses.

If you drummed your nails on the table so it rattled, little finger, ring finger, long finger, index finger, it sounded as if a rider were thundering past. The fingers jumped on the table. At first the sound was dry and then it grew softer and then he ran off into the distance.

I was embarrassed and hid my face in my cap when there was a love scene. I shut it out and held on to my cap by stretching the sweatband over my forehead and chin.

When I was sent to the movies in Alvik there was often a feeble-minded fat man over in the seventh row. He was completely round in the face and had a thin beard but slobbered and laughed and went around dressed like a child. He was harmless. Now and then he yelled, but no one paid any attention to him.

Olle and Lennart were not in a gang. I don't know why they didn't belong to one. Maybe it was because they couldn't get out of the house in the evening. Their mother kept track of what time they came home. They couldn't get out like I could, so they couldn't run around and be out with a gang.

Sometimes this was a problem. In February 1937 we built an ice castle at Olle and Lennart's house. We built it out of snow and made the wall smooth with water. It was not so much a castle as a model fortress. We had worked hard on it. In the evening when they were inside or maybe already in bed I was out with the gang. We were on our way up from the Olovslund stop. I didn't know where we were going. The leader hadn't said. When we went by the house where Olle and Lennart lived the redhead stopped and said:

"Have you ever seen such shit!"

Then we all went into the yard and kicked and pushed and went at it until the fortress was demolished and our work of several days was destroyed. It was heavy, sweaty work and had to be done quickly before anyone came out of the house. But we were able to smash it all and stamp on it. Then we all howled as loud as we could:

"Shit on you!"

And we all ran as fast as we could.

The next day Olle said someone had demolished our fortress. I said I thought that was sad and I really did think it was sad. I remember how we had worked to make a really fine fortress with towers and pinnacles and a flag at the very top. I was sorry about it. But I said nothing to Olle and Lennart about how I had taken part in kicking it apart and destroying it that night.

CHAPTER 29

From Gripsholms 400th anniversary I don't remember how the royal household guard's band, mounted on horses, played in the festivities or how the king came or how the governor spoke or what Arthur Engberg said. But I know I was there in the crowd watching. What I remember is that oxen were roasted on a spit and that I ate a whole fried oxen steak and that people danced in folk costumes.

The celebration lasted several days. Now forty-five years later I wonder if it really was the way I remember, that a whole roasted oxen was served to the people of Södermanland, or if what I remember was really an historical play. I could ask Aunt Karin. But I prefer the memory of the enormous meal. Maybe there was no individual meal—even if I do taste the good meat taste in my mouth as I write this—but a performance by touring actors and Mariefred neighbors in costume.

At the beginning of the summer I had been at Grandmother's. She was concerned about me. She sighed and washed me. She scrubbed me with a root brush. I had developed coarse, dark brown callouses on my elbows. Big flakes. Or you could say big horny flakes. Between them there were cracks that had started to bleed. She soaked them in warm water and scrubbed and kneaded cream into my elbows until they were smooth again. This always happened in the winter.

"I'm not saying anything," she said as she scrubbed me. I had been reading *The Three Musketeers*. Grandfather had bought it. It was a thick book bound in blue cloth from the Nordiska Förlag. I lay on my stomach under the table and read. When I looked up I could see myself in the big mirror with a gilded frame. It went from floor to ceiling. When Grandmother came in she said:

"You just read and read."

She took me out on walks. We went all the way to Kvicksta to visit. On the way there I picked a large bouquet of wildflowers. I was going to give it to my other Grandmother who was in Kvicksta and would offer me juice and cookies. When we were almost there Grandmother stepped off to the side:

"I'm going to piss," she said.

She said things like that. When someone was too finicky, she said:

"No one's such a shining star that she has never let a fart," she said. She said things like that. She used to see that I washed myself. She even washed me herself until I was ten. But if I became too concerned about cleanliness or wondered too much about what I was eating and peeled dirt and small bugs from berries before dropping them into my milk she said:

"A little dirt cleanses the stomach."

Robert and Greta and their children lived in Mariefred too. Robert was a teacher at Gripsholm Folk High School. But I didn't have much to do with them. Greta was refined. She was from a better family. She was born a Müntzing I think and always looked at me critically and made small unpleasant remarks. I kept my distance from her although she was an aunt.

Later I moved out to Kvicksta and was there the whole summer. I lived there several summers and sometimes also a few weeks during the winter. It was Grandfather's farm, but he and Grandmother lived mostly in their house outside Eskilstuna. Folke and Stig took care of the farm for him. Folke was the older and lived in a big house. It was from the seventeenth century. Stig, who was younger, lived in the small manager's house. I lived with Folke and Rosina in the big house but used to go down to eat with Stig and Karin. I could eat wherever I happened to be at mealtime. Everything was casual.

The road has been moved now. Before, it went across the stable yard and between the shed and the big house before it swung up through the pasture. Now it has been pulled directly across the swampy fields past all of Kvicksta.

We drive by there sometimes. We take the road through Kvicksta from Mariefred and on to Stallarholm. I see my window. We drive very close to it. Sometimes a light is on inside. I had the corner room toward the northwest. Outside it was the garden. But Kvicksta was sold during the war. Both Folke and Stig were called up for several years and Grandfather couldn't take care of the farm, and had to sell it. Before that they had built a house for Grandfather. It is further up on the slope when you have driven past Kvicksta.

The window was open so I heard the wind in the lindens when I lay on the floor and read and it was afternoon. It was one of Rosina's books. Big and heavy in brown with a gold globe on the middle of the cover. I read *Journey to the Center of the Earth* by Jules Verne and after getting lost I had come to Lidenbrock Sea. The broad seascape spread itself before my eyes. The black cliffs framed the view and from them the vast inside of the frame was lit by electricity in the air and by the lighthouse across the water.

But Axel was unnecessarily timid. A doubter. He caused problems. When he first heard of Arne Saknussem's secret entrance down to the center of the earth he tried to slow the journey down. And this despite the fact that he himself had participated in solving the riddle of the parchment.

Bees sang outside and the air was fragrant of summer. A fly buzzed at me. I swung at it with my hand to make it go away but it came even closer. A thunderstorm was coming. Everything was quiet and deep. Rosina came into the room and closed the window.

"You're reading," she said.

I wondered if the rain would reach here. You could often see the rain come far off above the edge of the woods. A gray curtain of rain which fell and came closer and then the rain parted and Kvicksta remained dry despite the soaking all around.

"The farm is in an unlucky place," said Folke.

When the rumbling came closer and it began to get too dark to read I went out to the living room. There I could stand in the middle of the floor and look out over the fields toward the woods on the other side. It was like a huge theater scene. Now the clouds were blue-black above the woods and the white curtains moved in the draft from the window. Then came the first crack of thunder. It was not very far away. I had been able to count seven seconds from the first flash of lightning against the black clouds until the thunder came. It blew out the switches. Blue-white sparks flew and lightning struck very close, followed almost immediately by thunder. Now it was above us and this time the rain poured down and beat on the windowpanes. Flames lit the field scene and it thundered so the house shook and I was very happy. The air tasted different now that the thunderstorm had passed and a magnificent panorama spread itself out before me when I looked out at the landscape. The huge frame was lit by electricity in the air and through the veil of rain.

I had learned to close the window properly and shut the heat registers so lightning would not be drawn into the room. Grandmother used to tell about balls of lightning that rolled through the room. I had never seen that myself. That wouldn't be until 1941 when I lived with Elsa and Gösta at Viggeby. Then a ball of lightning hissed through the room. It came out of the wall switches and was a blue-white ball, a globe, a balloon that went first here then there and left black tracks after itself until it went out the open door into the kitchen where it disappeared. But I wasn't afraid even then. It was only exciting. Although others were frightened, and some so frightened that they broke into a cold sweat in a thunderstorm, I always thought it was fun. There was a certain joy in seeing lightning, hearing thunder and feeling the hairs on your neck spark and tingle.

Afterward I went out. The gravel in the courtyard was wet. I could pick it up with my toes and toss it away. The air was cool, almost chilly. Birds talked to each other after the storm and I crept into the kennel with Träff, though there was almost no space. He smelled of wet dog and made room for me. I thought about wandering down through the long passages from the crater in Snaefel Glacier to the Lidenbrock Sea, where the vast inner space was lit by the flickering light of electricity and where the whole world continued to live on for eons.

CHAPTER 30

Folke didn't talk much to me. For the most part he walked quietly and thought. He said:

"Listen, you little devil, close the gate properly." He used the same tone when he talked to me and when he talked to Träff.

"Listen, you damn dog," he said.

It wasn't swearing. It was like when the actor Fridolf Rhudin said:

"I'm the dog of the house."

I got to go along when Folke went into the woods. I got to go along when he drove the milk to the dairy in Stallarholm. He lifted the back seat out of the old Ford and then it was like a delivery van. He loaded the milk and drove. On the way he picked up milk from the small farms too. The big farms drove their own milk to the dairy.

My two thumbs are different. The right one is longer. It has a different kind of nail. It looks like the thumbs belong to two different people. That is because I got my right thumb stuck in the car door at Ulriksdal. I had climbed in and was still holding on to the handle when Folke slammed the door. It hurt. But I didn't scream. That was not done. After a moment, when I could begin to speak, I said:

"My thumb seems to be a little bit stuck. Could you open the door?"

I almost didn't get the whole sentence out, it hurt so much. It took a little time to think it through, but afterward I decided it could have been better. Grettir would have said it more dryly. I got *Grettir's Saga* from Gösta. It was Hjalmar Alving's translation of the book and already just about read to pieces. I got a chill when I came to the end of the saga and Styrla Lawgiver summarized Grettir's life. I looked at Folke and tried to look untroubled.

"My thumb is in a bit of a jam," I said.

Folke looked at me. Then he got out of the car and opened the door. I took my thumb out. It was bloody and torn. Folke looked at it.

"We'd better turn around and go home," he said.

"That's not necessary," I said.

We drove back to Kvicksta later. Folke had given me his handkerchief so I wouldn't bleed so much.

When we got home Rosina filled a whole drinking glass with hydrogen peroxide and I stuck my thumb in it. It hurt so much I almost blacked out and my eyes watered and it was difficult to breathe normally and pretend nothing was wrong.

"Does it hurt much?" asked Rosina.

"It's not too bad," I said.

Now the thumb turned white and various pieces of skin fell off. The nail fell off too and I had to go with a bandage on my thumb the whole summer.

Gunnar got a look at my thumb at Christmas that year. It had grown a coarse yellow deformed nail. It was flat too.

"You need to hide that thumb when we get to America," he said. "Otherwise the immigration authorities will think you have syphilis and they'll send you home again." Then he laughed. I really did keep that thumb properly hidden when we passed through customs in New York in the fall of 1938.

Folke had a workshop in the shed. He repaired tools there. He also made a model boat for me. One day he said:

"We could build a little motorboat. A model. What do you say?"

I nodded.

"OK, then, little devil," said Folke, "we'll do it."

It turned out to be a beautiful model. It was almost twenty inches long. It had slim lines and a real planing hull. While he worked on it, Folke talked to me now and then. I got to hold the tools and take care of the gluepot.

In the fall when I had to leave Kvicksta and move to Elsa and Gösta's house in Sigtuna, where I was to live until winter vacation, Folke said:

"Next year we'll paint it and put in a little steam engine."

But it didn't work out that way. The next year the boat was gone and I don't know what happened to it. But it was very pretty to look at and the wood was sandpapered smooth that fall of 1937.

CHAPTER 31

I collected pictures. I had a large series of pirate pictures from chewing gum. I traded my doubloons. I had several copies of the map of an island with buried treasure and when I biked down to the Olovslund stop to buy new pirate gum, I sang:

> "Thirteen men on a dead man's chest
> Yo ho ho and a bottle of rum."

In a blue scrapbook I pasted pictures of cars and car engines clipped from newspapers. I sat in my room on Thaliavägen in the afternoons and clipped and pasted. I had a whole section on Fords in the book. They weren't exciting cars but they were nice in their own way. The Ford V8 Coupe de Luxe was no ordinary car and it almost had what it took. Even the Ford Junior could play luxury model sports car in luxury edition. It was open-topped.

But the cars that interested me the most were Delage and Amilcar and even Rolls Royce. They had different lines. And I liked the Wanderer. The sport model had double spare tires back in the trunk. It had an electrical gas pump too. The twelve cylinder Horch was a stylish car.

But is wasn't just a question of lines. I was a passionate advocate of front wheel drive. Horses do not push carts in front of themselves! Cars like the Brennabors six-cylinder sport limousine and the Stoewer got many pages. The Stoewer looked almost like a boxy and boring old Ford or Volvo. But it was smaller and had only two doors. The design was beautiful when you looked at the chassis. It was like that because the motor and driveshaft were a single unit and only the battery was back above the rear axel.

With a large Meccano set you could build a Bentley chassis. I had only a small Meccano. To build a chassis for the Bentley six-cylinder three-and-a-half-liter engine you needed the L set. It was very large. But if you built the chassis it was almost like a real one. All the pedals worked. The steering was like a real car and the wheels tilted outward as they should and the transmission had four forward gears and one reverse. It was a wonderful transmission. I cut out the picture and thought about how the cogwheels hummed and gripped each other and made a thick red frame around it.

If you had an L set maybe you could build a chassis like that first, just to learn to build, and then build a Stoewer chassis. I tried to think how a Stoewer chassis could be built. I had no really good pictures of the crucial parts. But it was probably possible to figure it out.

I went down to talk to Gunnar about it one day. I had prepared myself for a long time. I knew what he would say, but on the other hand I had to at least try. I talked to him about the chassis and Meccano set L.

"Yes, that's good," he said. "Now go play with your Meccano."

I tried to explain that I meant a bigger Meccano.

"You're crazy," he said.

Then he waved me off. At least he had not said any more than "No."

I got *The Motorcycle Handbook* from Folke. Folke had driven a motorcycle years ago. There were beautiful pictures of engines. In general, motorcycles were good because you could really see the engines. They were not hidden behind sheet metal. Where motorcycles were concerned I was most interested in reintroducing power transmission by axel and cogwheel. Chains—not to mention belts—were not really very engine-like, although almost all of them had chains. But the old F N from Belgium had axels and cogwheel and now the Germans were beginning to do that again.

A J S were good machines too. One of the smaller ones would be enough. There was no need for a two-cylinder thousand-cubic. A 350 with vents and double exhaust pipes was plenty.

I didn't clip pictures only of cars and motorcycles. I clipped other pictures too. I kept them hidden in a folder behind my cut-out theater. I had built it and glued it together and you could perform different plays on its stage and pull the curtain and everything. It was not as much fun to play theater as it was to build a theater.

Alva came in the door one afternoon when I was clipping pictures out of *Vecko-Journalen*.

"What are you doing?" she asked.

"Nothing," I said.

"But what are you cutting?" she asked.

"Dolls for the theater," I said.

She stood quietly a while behind me and I felt in my neck that she was looking at me. Then she left and closed the door after herself.

I was cutting out girls in lingerie from advertisements and they were not at all for theaters. I was aroused by them. That began when I lived on Thaliavägen.

We sat in a circle in the bushes on the vacant lot down by the streetcar. They said no one wanted to build there because someone high up in Stockholm Streetcars had the idea you could keep frost away by mixing salt with gravel. They had done that and all the salt had leaked out and polluted the lots and no one wanted the salty lots. In any case we sat in a circle and jerked each other off. I remember that very clearly and have remembered it for a long time because it was the only time I ever jerked off another boy. It was the leader who suggested it and each of us jerked off the one who sat to the right. There were probably ten of us.

Up in my room on Thaliavägen we used to jerk off when we played. But we didn't jerk each other off. We thought up fantasies and jerked off. We were pilots going out on our last mission and before we flew away we fucked our wives.

We biked down to Ålsten one Sunday morning just before school was out. We looked for condoms. Down at the water we found one and then another. The water was almost warm enough for swimming. We put on the used condoms and masturbated. We said they were girls who had come to us in the woods and we fucked them.

In the summer when we were cutting hay at Kvicksta we played and jumped in the hay. There was a girl there wearing a blue dress. I don't think she was from the farm. I don't remember her except that day. She might have been visiting. She was about the same age as I. Maybe a year older, eleven or so. She and I jumped and she told a story about a boy at Länna who had jumped in the hay and didn't see that he was jumping on a stake. He got the stake all the way through him and it stuck out his back and he died the next day.

She had frizzy hair and screwed her eyes when she laughed. When we were alone in the hay she said:

"Now I'm going to milk a cow."

She stuck her finger down my pants and began to rub me. We lay in the hay and it was fragrant and soft. Then I touched her cunt and I had her whole cunt under my hand and she closed her eyes.

Then Folke called from below.

"Damn rascal! Are you there? Rosina is waiting with lunch."

The girl jumped away and then I climbed down. I didn't want anyone to see what had been going on.

"You're playing in the hay," said Folke.

"Yes," I said.

"Don't hurt yourself," said Folke. "There was a boy near here who jumped on a stake and killed himself.

I looked for the girl the next afternoon, but she had already left. I thought about her a lot. It would be several years before I got so close to a girl again. At Christmas that year I was taken to Stockholm for the holidays and stayed at a small hotel on Grönviksvägen. I do not remember where Alva and Gunnar were with my sisters. In any case, I shared a room with Mary. I slept in an alcove in the room. In the evening when it was dark I masturbated and thought about the girl in the hay and saw her. I tried to masturbate so Mary would not hear and breathed carefully and quietly. She heard anyway and asked:

"Jan! What are you doing?"

"Nothing," I said.

CHAPTER 32

In the fall of 1937 I was with Elsa and Gösta in Sigtuna. Alva and Gunnar had left Thaliavägen. The owner of the house was coming back. Markelius had designed a house for them. It was to be built on Nyängsvägen right in front of Bromma Secondary School.

Elsa and Gösta were elementary school teachers. Elsa was my father's sister. She taught at Sigtuna Elementary School and I went there too, but wasn't in her class. My teacher's name was Andeby. The only thing I really remember of him was that he told Elsa he didn't understand what they meant when they said I was a problem child.

"He's just a regular boy, rowdy like the others." Elsa agreed with him. They sat in the room and talked and I listened at the door. I didn't sneak in there to listen to them. I had just happened to come by and when I heard them talk about me I stopped to listen.

I liked Gösta. I always had. Even at Gesta when he was engaged to Elsa he took me out on walks and told me about geological formations and inland ice. Later, during the war when Alva and Gunnar stayed in America and sent me to Sweden, and Grandmother took care of me and my sisters even though she was getting old, Gösta was my guardian.

Now that I lived with Elsa and Gösta he would talk to me in the evenings and on Sundays. He made a hectograph for me. In the kitchen we poured the warm yellow mass into a mould. I think it consisted of glue and glycerine. In any case it smelled of glue.

Gösta played marbles with me too. He was an expert at

that. He could send a slow one right into a pyramid of marbles all the way from the other end of the yard. He had actually been a soccer player.

Before Sunday dinner he went out with his daughter Majt and me and looked at ruins. He talked about Ansgar and Christianity and the Kingdom of the Swedes and he did it in a different way from other teachers. He was a very good teacher. I know that now. Even after retirement he continued to work as a teacher of particularly difficult students. He had trouble walking then after he hurt his hip and was frail. But even tall ungainly boys who had knocked down policemen with a single blow and were considered totally incorrigible became docile and mild when he looked at them. They never lifted a finger against him and never raised their voices when he told them to be quiet. Now that he is dead they come to me and talk about him.

We took long walks on Sundays and he showed me the levels of clay and showed how each level consisted of a lighter and a darker layer. The dark had been set during the winter and the light during the summer when the water streamed out and laid layer on layer year after year so you could count down through the years. It was during the post-glacial era ten thousand years ago.

He told how Sweden had been after the ice age. He talked about the tundra and all the everyday birds in the springtime and how the first people came wandering up. They were hunters. There might have been people before the ice age, even up here, but nothing was known about them. It was impossible to know anything about them because the ice had gone across the land like a massive shovel and scraped away everything that was loose and pressed it into a mountain. Now the ice was gone and the mountain began to rise. It rose slowly because everything goes slowly in geological time but the land continued to rise. Where the Vikings had launched their ships, there were now fields and meadows and just where we were walking a dragon ship had gone out and the men had raised their shields and yelled.

When we got home we got roast veal with small round potatoes and glazed carrots and gravy and black currant jelly.

Late that fall I heard that Gunnar and Alva were going to America next year to solve the Negro problem and they were taking me along. But I was not to tell anyone.

I used to go to Sigtuna Foundation Library. There I borrowed as if I were an adult. The woman in charge was the bishop's sister. I looked through the shelves for books about America and finally had to ask her. She helped me take down various books about America's geography and I read about its geology and mountains and rivers and cities and looked at pictures of Chicago and New York and St. Louis. She wondered why I was so interested in America and then I happened to say that I might be going there. I don't think I said much more than that, but two days later the newspaper said Gunnar was going to America and I was afraid I had said too much. One should never say anything to anyone.

But I continued to go to the library because it was the best one I had ever been in. Late that fall I started to read Flammarion. My favorite was his *Wonders of the Atmosphere*. It used old-fashioned spelling but that didn't matter to me. The library had Jules Verne too.

I sat at the window and outside the rain was gray over the fields and the woods were a dark mass in the gray rain. I read about mirages and haloes and counter-suns and how cloud masses look from a balloon (and on July 4, 1873, the balloon of the unfortunate aeronaut La Mountain lost its gondola and he landed in the marshes with a soft thud and the body went six inches into the ground).

Rain fell and that rain might have been the same water which carried the dragon ship because everything was a circle and what we breathe, drink and eat had already been breathed, drunk and eaten millions of times. Dead or alive, we are made of the same materials in the eternal circle of creatures and things.

It got dark and I imagined an absolutely free globe, not attached to anything and with no supports upon which to rest, flung out into endless space. It was the center and unity of the universe, the world's up and down, left and right and at the same time just one of millions of bodies in the endlessness of space. Now it was completely dark in the room and outside the rain could be heard and I tried one more time to see our globe rush forward into limitlessness borne by the general mystical laws of gravity. There was an almost melancholy longing sweetness throughout the body and Flammarion concludes that living intellectually increases the joy of living tenfold and that we leave to others flesh and its desires and we choose the spirit and its enjoyment.

Soon it would be 1938 and I would turn eleven years old and travel to America and leave Sigtuna Elementary School and Sweden. At night I saw the girl in the hay. She had suntanned legs and I took her by the crotch and masturbated quietly so no one would hear.

ABOUT THE AUTHOR

JAN MYRDAL is the author of more than 60 books—political and social commentary, literary and art criticism, history, novels, plays, and poetry. He has also edited scholarly editions of Strindberg and Balzac, curated exhibitions, made feature films and numerous television documentaries. Very few of these have appeared in English, and he is best known in the United States and England for his *Confessions of a Disloyal European* and *Report from a Chinese Village.*

The second book in his childhood series, *Another World,* was awarded the Great Prize for the Novel of the Literature Foundation, and the third book, *Twelve Going on Thirteen,* was awarded the Esselte Prize for Literature, with 100,000 copies distributed to Sweden's middle school seniors.

Jan Myrdal was recently honored by the French Government as a Chevalier des arts et des lettres. He maintains his controversial presence on the Swedish cultural scene through frequent newspaper articles and appearances on radio and television.